Laughing & Learning

David Middlewood

First published in Great Britain as a softback original in 2021

Copyright © David Middlewood

The moral right of this author has been asserted.

All rights reserved.

No part of this publication may be reproduced, stored in a retrieval system, or transmitted, in any form or by any means, without the prior permission in writing of the publisher, nor be otherwise circulated in any form of binding or cover other than that in which it is published and without a similar condition including this condition being imposed on the subsequent purchaser.

Typeset in Minion Pro

Editing, design, typesetting and publishing by UK Book Publishing

www.ukbookpublishing.com

ISBN: 978-1-914195-73-0

CONTENTS

PART A: PRIMARY CONCERNS 1

    Chapter 1: Days of Innocence 2
    Chapter 2: Those In-between Years 27

PART B: THE OTHER SIDE OF THE DESK 59

    Chapter 3: First Steps 60
    Chapter 4: Something A Little More Senior 86
    Chapter 5: It's Tough At The Top! 107

PART C: IT'S ALL ACADEMIC ANYWAY 135

    Chapter 6: Among the great and good? 136
    Chapter 7: A brief look back-and forward 166

PART A
PRIMARY CONCERNS

Chapter One

DAYS OF INNOCENCE

I think perhaps I first realised that I might want to be a teacher when I discovered at the age of about eight that teachers really do have eyes in the back of their heads. I believed it to be one of those peculiarities of certain groups of people. Just as witches were known to have three nipples, so teachers apparently did have at least one extra eye in the back of the head. I found this out at my village primary school and, although I knew I did not have that extra eye then, I thought it might be something that grew as you became a teacher. Actually, I think this may still be true – except not quite so literally, of course. I felt, however, as I matured a little that I might have something that could prove a significant handicap if I did want to be a teacher – I had a strong, and some say weird, sense of humour!

You see, a habit of mine that I confess in adulthood I have found difficult to break is that I will often respond to a harmless inquiry with a quip, or some kind of humorous remark. I hope I know when to be serious

CHAPTER ONE

and that I have always been a committed educational professional, but it is hard sometimes to stop the humour breaking in. When a secretary at one of the universities I worked for asked me in preparing for a trip whether I had a list, I felt almost compelled to answer: 'No, I always walk like this!' I only used that one once, of course!

When a group of newly graduated MA students asked me, knowing my retirement was looming, whether I was going to go on the stage, I think it was intended as a compliment! Having spent all my working life and therefore the vast majority of my life to date in the world of education, I have more recently found some time to reflect on the lighter aspects of that world which is of such great importance to everyone and one which brings such huge rewards to so many. Particularly, I have been recalling so many of the odd, quirky and downright funny things that have happened to me and others in this world. The crucial thing that both bedevils and enhances working in education is that EVERYONE knows something about it. Everybody, after all, has experience of education – and many are often only too ready to pass on their knowledge of it to you, whether you have asked for it or not. Ask most people what they remember about their school days, and, among the most vivid memories, there are more than likely to be humorous incidents with a teacher or classmate. Two incidents in my own recent past have reminded me of some of the rewards in teaching, each with a humorous side, but with other meaning perhaps.

In the first, I was walking the two miles back home from the garage where I had left my car for its service, when I passed a lorry with the men collecting household rubbish from bins. One of them, aged about thirty, came running up to me and waving and calling out:

'It's Mister Middlewood, isn't it?'

'That's right.'

'You used to be my old head when I was at secondary school.'

I acknowledged this and apologised that I didn't remember him personally but there had been a lot of students, etc.

'Oh, that's okay. I was always in trouble anyway there, but you were okay. You were fair.'

Assuming that by 'fair', he was referring to my sense of justice and not to my overall performance as a school leader, I asked him how he found life these days.

'Oh, I'm doing fine – got a place of my own – I'm married with two kids now – and–', he paused, before adding in triumph, 'I've only had one ABH since I left school!'

Having been the head of a school for young people of all backgrounds and abilities, I had enough experience of course to know that ABH stood for a criminal offence, meaning causing 'Actual Bodily Harm'! We parted very amicably, and as I walked on, I reflected on how, during my long career in education, I had taught people who had gone on to be BAs, BScs, BEds, MAs, MEds, MScs, and even DDs and PhDs, but I doubt whether any of them had greeted me more enthusiastically than this single ABH had! Furthermore, the job he was doing for people like me was as valuable as anything those others had probably done, especially perhaps during the circumstances of the pandemic of 2020 and 2021.

The second episode involved a chance meeting with a somewhat older man whom I encountered by chance on a platform at Coventry Rail

CHAPTER ONE

Station. We discovered, while studying the same train timetable, that we had been at the same school in Kent in the mid-1970s where I taught English and had in fact been Head of English.

'I thought I recognised you from a long time back. Mister Middlewood, isn't it?'

'That's right!'

'You know, it's funny but after all these years I still remember some of those lessons when I did English Lit. at GCE 'O' level. Henry the Fourth Part something.'

'Part One, that would be.'

'I knew you'd know! That Prince Hal – he was a right tearaway, he was!'

I agreed with him that Prince Hal had indeed been a 'right tearaway', and said how pleased I was that he recalled it all.

'Well,' he said, 'I don't know about 'all of it', of course, but I have a lad now who is about sixteen and he is turning into, well, just like that, and it made me think about how in the end, so you told us, he turned out okay.'

'Yes, that's sort of at the end of Part Two,' I said, and I went on to reassure him I knew quite a bit from real life about sixteen-year-old tearaways, as well as from Shakespeare.

'There was that old fat drunk chap too, always exaggerating! You made us laugh a lot about that.'

I modestly pointed out that the credit for Falstaff's behaviour was really William Shakespeare's, but again said how pleased I was it had stayed with him. My train then arrived and we had no more time, but again, I was left to reflect on how we never know for certain the impact of some aspects of education and teaching, but obviously those scenes we enacted together in class while studying Shakespeare's play for his exam had stayed with that man. I remembered getting them all in that class to build up a picture of telling a highly exaggerated story like Falstaff's in the play. They then mimicked me and I did the same with them, although being careful to observe professional discretion when they turned to mimicking other teachers of course!

As a student and then as a teacher of English, I have always been both an obsessive reader and a writer, or at the very least a scribbler. Teaching English in schools enabled me to indulge my reading and make it my work, and the final stage of my working life working in Higher Education brought the chance to write professionally and actually have it published!

My first indulgence after finally retiring from any form of teaching was to write and publish a book of my poems, written from the 1980s onwards. These included a few humorous poems which seemed popular with various readers. In my now slightly more leisurely life, I became involved with, among other things, a nursing home very near to my own home where I have lived with my wife since 1985. This link was strengthened when I found out the manager, now a good friend, had briefly been a sixth form student in the school where I had been Head! The residents there soon discovered my love of reading and poetry and very soon I was dubbed 'David the Bard', and it was a requirement on me from the residents to produce a limerick for them each time I visited – saucy but not too rude! I have recently written one for a resident lady for her hundredth birthday! Limericks later played an

CHAPTER ONE

important part in my teacher training, by the way! My wife and I also produced various entertainments for the home, and on top of that I then received an invitation to show the comic side of Higher Education by contributing to an international publication on that topic (Thank you, Kishor Vaidya!).

The more I reflected on the various funny incidents involving myself and friends and colleagues, the more I realised just how much humour there is and has been in working in education. Do not get me wrong – I hope and I believe that I have always been a dedicated and serious professional educationalist; but without laughter, smiles and humour, how would any of us working in education survive? As I write this in my room at home, there is beside me a presentation gift from some Master's Degree Students in the Seychelles, all mature teachers therefore. The gift's actual rather cheeky form will be described later, but its inscription reads:

'Presented to David Middlewood by his grateful Seychelles MA students for his wonderful work – and humour.'

It is those final two words that have encouraged me to write this much longer account of the humorous side of my life in education. It is, of course, a highly selective account, because I have, like anyone else with a lifetime in education, had many periods of sheer hard work, occasional setbacks, heartaches, even tragedies, and a few periods of boredom; but throughout it all a really rewarding commitment to those I worked with and for, teachers and learners alike. I believe we are all both of these at various times in our lives, and that no really effective learning takes place without enjoyment.

All the incidents that are described in this book are ones that did actually happen, but the names have been changed, apart from those of a few friends who have been happy for me to mention them personally. What we nearly all have in common is working in education and the belief that it only works when the teaching and learning is enjoyable for at least some of the time.

So, when does one decide to become a teacher? Or is it decided for you, perhaps? In my case, I need to go right back to the beginning…

It is well known that the single most significant period of human life for learning is that of the first three years. In no other time do we humans take such huge strides in our development – while we play, we learn! When someone has spent virtually all their life in learning and teaching, perhaps researching and writing about this, it must be very disconcerting if you can personally remember nothing of those years! Fortunately for me, memories of my childhood, including some of its very early days, are quite vivid. In that small village in rural Kent, living in a tumbledown 'cottage' with only very basic amenities (no hot water and initially no electricity!), about three quarters of a mile from the school and church, I enjoyed a happy and fairly unrestrained upbringing with my mother and my sister, Daphne, four years older than me. My father I have no recollection of until his 'demob' and homecoming in August 1945. My wife, Jacqui, herself a city girl, has described my childhood as compared with hers for example as one of 'healthy neglect', and that seems to me a very fair description, noting that the 'healthy' implied a large helping of maternal love. As far as I am concerned, we were a single parent family till my father's homecoming, just like so many others around us. I do remember the actual day my father came home from his wartime service, because he sat on my newly completed jigsaw! Even now, I resent him having done that and wish I could dismiss the memory, but every time I look at a photograph of him in his army uniform, I cannot help thinking of that jigsaw and wondering what happened to those lost pieces! I did not know in those

CHAPTER ONE

very early days much about this place called 'school' and what it meant, except that my sister apparently went there daily with her friend from next door and told me that one day my turn would come.

It did come, of course, just about, as I realised later, as the Second World War was ending, and I began there at the Easter before I was five in October. The powers that be were not as punctilious then as now about enrolment dates, and this early start stayed with me throughout my school and university days, as will be told. Disappointingly, I have no striking memories of my very first day, and I have read Laurie Lee's account of his first day at school with enjoyment and with envy – how he was told to sit there 'for the present', and got upset when his present never arrived! Nothing as memorable as his initiation occurred to me, but I do vaguely recall in the first month or so being pushed through the gap in the playground railings into the adjoining orchard, as was the fate of all new children it seemed, in order to scrump some unripe fruit to bring back for the older boys. The only reward for this exploit seemed to be stomach-ache and even perhaps occasional diarrhoea.

My first encounter with the realities of educational institutions and their culture, structures and strategies that I was much later to write about came in my first fortnight. I realised later that it must have been an alarm drill practice, because, although Kent had taken a fearsome battering from the dreaded doodlebugs a few years earlier, that would have long ceased by this time. Be that as it may, the alarm bell sounded, and everyone was ordered to leave the classrooms and make their way to the shelter in the playground. There was to be no messing about and no talking!

So, off we all went, the newly arrived and the old lags together, holding hands in a line into the pitch black of the brick-built and asphalt-roofed shelter. Apart from the odd whimper and sniffle, I heard and felt nothing until the all-clear bell rang and we all trooped dutifully back to our class. But it was NOT, as I supposed, all over! Barely had we arrived back in the Infants' classroom, when Mrs Dutton, the headmistress, walked into the Infants' room and announced that all boys must come – NOW! – to the other room where the older children were taught. We boys assembled there, along with the older boys and were told to form a line. Mystified, as I could see other boys in the infants class also were, I wondered what part of the wartime strategy this could be.

'Now,' said Mrs Dutton, looking sternly up and down the line, 'what I want to know is–' She paused, and I desperately tried to imagine what possible act of wartime treachery had been carried out.

'–which of you boys pulled Ann Linfield's knickers down when we were in the shelter? Come on, own up, whoever you are!'

This took me by surprise, not so much initially as to the potential injustice of this accusation as far as I was concerned, but at the peculiar problem as to WHY anyone should pull anyone else's knickers down. To my four and two thirds year old mind, this was surely the key question – not who, but why? Why would a boy want a girl's knickers? Of course, I knew what knickers were – after all, I had a sister. I knew the two basic things about knickers even at that age –firstly, only girls wore them, and secondly, they were all navy blue! Briefly, an idea flashed into my mind – was the headmistress wrong in assuming it was a boy? Perhaps there was a girl who was envious of Ann's particular pair and had in the dark sought to steal them or even exchange them for a more ragged and worn pair? There were certainly girls in the village who, judging by their outward appearance, would have owned and worn ragged underwear, whereas Ann, whom I had already met in my infants class, was a relatively smartly dressed young girl. I believe I was formulating this theory when I realised that Mrs Dutton was standing in front of

CHAPTER ONE

me, as she worked her way down the line.

'And you, David? Was it you?'

I stammered out my denial, forgetting my theory utterly. She came to the last boy, and received the final denial.

'Right! All you boys – hold out your hands, flat open.'

We all did so, and down the line she came, giving a smart slap with a ruler on each palm extended. I had a feeling her blows were much harder on the older boys' palms than on us infants, but I cannot be sure of this. I only know it did not actually hurt much at all. The mystery, of course, remained unsolved, but my own theory that the criminal was Bob, the older brother of my friend Doug, was based on what seemed to me three pretty strong pieces of evidence: namely, the grin on his face as the smacking ended, his general reputation as a scallywag, and of course the fact that he bragged incessantly about having done it for weeks afterwards!

As years passed, I realised there had been nothing remotely sexual about this incident, something confirmed by Ann herself when we travelled home on the bus together from our respective grammar schools many years later. We were about fourteen years old at this time, but both remembered the incident vividly. According to Ann, being plunged into the sudden darkness of the shelter startled her so much that she, as she put it, 'desperately wanted a wee', and said so aloud. Whereupon a nearby boy said something to the effect that 'You'll need these down then!' and gave her knickers a yank.

'I probably made a fuss,' Ann said, 'but I was only five!'

I am not sure what I replied on this later occasion, as at 14 years old, female underwear was a topic normally only discussed with male friends of the same age, and in quite different terms.

Thus was my first encounter with some of the key principles of schooling that I have written about in published academic tomes, such as discipline, equity, gender equality, school ethos and leadership.

There were just two teachers initially in the school, later expanded to three when I was about eight years old. All were female and none of them lived in the village, travelling instead by daily bus from the small town about four miles away. Mrs Dutton had taken over as Headmistress just before I began school. I knew this because my sister had had a Mr Barton, known as 'Mad Johnny' in the village, as her headteacher. I was not sure of the origin of his nickname, but stories about him and his feud with the village parson, 'Gobby' March, were legendary. One story involved the two of them squaring up to each other in the school playground over the parson's insistence on his coming into this 'church school' (it certainly was a 'C of E' school) and the headteacher disputing this right. The rumour was that a young woman called Daisy also played a key role in the row between the two men, but I know no more. As I grew older, I often wondered about this possible femme fatale and her identity. However, there were at least four and probably more women in the village who were called Daisy, so the truth was never to be discovered by me. As an adolescent, I pondered the possible relative merits of each of these middle-aged Daisies and their likelihood for the earlier role as a village harlot, but to my mind at that age, none seemed a very likely candidate.

The bias of having an all-female staff at the school showed itself in various ways, including the fact that in Physical Education (PE), the activities were, as it seemed to us boys, particularly 'girlie'. One bias I

CHAPTER ONE

recall was that in playing leapfrog in official PE lessons, the boys always had to make the back while the girls jumped over. I can still feel a kind of breathlessness recalling lying collapsed on the asphalt surface underneath a very large girl called Pamela. This was not in any way caused by a kind of breathtaking excitement at the inter-gender contact, but simply that every bit of wind in my body had been squeezed out of me by Pamela's considerable bulk. In fairness to her, I should mention that Pam developed into rather an attractive young female in her teens with a very fetching figure, at a time when I would have quite welcomed being squashed by her – though, alas, it was not to be. Needless to say, out of school this particular practice in leapfrogging was not adhered to and both sexes were equally happy to take turns at the more exciting and exacting role in the game.

However, when it came to real games, the matter was more serious. Somehow, the school possessed two netball posts and thus netball became the game which all of us were obliged to play. We all enjoyed it, girls and boys, but of course it was not football – which is what in winter we boys spent every spare minute involved in, whether kicking a tennis ball, a rubber ball or indeed any kind of relatively soft spherical object. The boys' grumblings and mutterings obviously eventually got through to Mrs Dutton, because one memorable day, when the time came for playground PE, she summoned us together.

'Now, you boys,' she said, holding a large shopping bag in one hand. 'I am a little tired of your complaining about always playing netball. So—'

She reached into the large shopping bag and produced – a new football! It was very small but undeniably a real football with the leather panels that showed its authenticity. It was shiny new too.

We were ready to throw ourselves at her feet to worship her benevolence, and almost slavering at the sight of this new heavenly gift, but our headmistress was not finished.

'This is for the boys of this school; as you can see, it is brand new and wonderfully clean. So, woe betide any of you if you get it dirty!'

Stunned silence followed. Did this woman know nothing of the basic nature of football? That one of the essences of the game was to dribble through mud, to tackle someone in competing for the ball and bring them crashing down in the grime? Given that our 'turf' was the meadow over the road and opposite to the school, where the other occupants between any games were cows – and cows have a habit of leaving their own distinctive markings on any pitch – was she mad? However, we nodded our agreement, seized the ball and rushed off to play under her watchful eye. We had the good sense, while she was still watching, to play at heading the ball only, where the rule was that the ball must not touch the ground. As soon as she was out of sight, of course, a 'proper' game was able to ensue. It had to be in the meadow, naturally, as the playground might have scratched the sacred surface of the ball.

Gradually we developed a ritual whereby the specific task of one boy (we took it in turns) at the end of the game was to religiously wipe and clean the ball with whatever material could be found. We brought various old and well used cloths from home, with an occasional boy getting into trouble at home for purloining the household's main towel; but the worst problem, which I remember only too well on one occasion when it was my turn to clean, were those cows and their deposits! During a game, wiping the ball on the grass was sufficient, but cleaning it into immaculate condition at the end before it was returned to the headmistress took painstaking care, a rendering of the cloth as unusable ever again, and a good deal of mirth from the other players!

CHAPTER ONE

Eventually, of course, Mrs Dutton lost interest and accepted wear and tear – and a bit of dirt – on the ball as normal, but her introduction to the game has stayed with me. On reflection, I have wondered if there was some cunning strategy behind her instruction not to make the ball dirty. Certainly, when much later we played against others, our heading seemed to be one of our key strengths as a team!

The large meadow opposite the school, which contained our football pitch-cowpats and all, was also used for various other activities. At the May festival, the children would be forced to re-locate to the village recreation ground – or 'the rec' as we knew it – about half a mile away, because parents could hardly be asked to run the risk of standing in a cow pat whilst watching any maypole dancing. It was strange how many of the older boys seemed to suffer an injury to an ankle or knee in the period leading up to a maypole dance display, and therefore be unavailable for the dancing, while the girls remained remarkably free from injury.

One custom I do recall, though, which was exclusively held in the meadow took place at Easter. The smaller children were invited to hunt for Easter eggs around the base of the huge tree which stood in the corner of the meadow nearest the school. These eggs were real ones donated by local farmers, hard boiled, and then painted by the older children and teachers. Only one egg per child was allowed, naturally. As usual, a joker made a mark one year by including an egg which was not boiled at all, but had somehow been smuggled into the number hidden around the tree. The smile on the face of one small child quickly turned to astonishment when he was invited to throw it up in the air and catch it, as hard boiled ones often were. A slightly suspicious Mrs Dutton reached out her hand to catch the egg for the child and found a sticky mess trickling down her arm – to huge giggles from all those around. I am sure she found the guilty party in her normal way, and administered the general punishment accordingly. As it happened, since I was on that occasion of the age to be among the small recipients of the eggs, I was at least this time free from any such retribution.

Village schools such as mine were, one realises, just about as comprehensive and mixed-ability (to use later educationally fashionable terms) as it was possible to be. In fact, many of them still are, I am sure. Certainly, even those village primary schools in the English rural shires that I visited in the 1990s while working for Leicester University had truly mixed intakes of pupils. In fact, working in the smallest ones where only one, or at the most two, classes existed was regarded then as one of the toughest jobs in education because teachers had to cope with teaching children from across more than one of what had become by then rigidly structured 'Key Stages' – all in the same class. Additionally, I have had the experiences of both my wife, Jacqui, and my eldest son, Gavin, to draw on, as they have both taught in such primary schools at different times. Likewise, the small rural schools I visited for research purposes in that same period, and later, in places such as South Africa, Tanzania, Seychelles in Africa and Greece in Europe had similar characteristics.

In the same classroom in such schools, just like mine in the late 1940s, might sit a tiny number of children destined for university later in life; a number who would attain a reasonable standard and go on to lead satisfactory lives and careers; a small number who struggled with, or were hostile to, the kind of learning on offer; and a very small number incapable of learning virtually anything of that kind because of genetic, physical or mental deficiencies. Today, we recognise that final category as those with 'special educational needs' (SEN) or 'learning problems' or learning disabilities. That group has been through a whole range of descriptions during my lifetime in education ('slow learners' and 'remedial' being just two of the official terms at different stages; in one

CHAPTER ONE

infamous secondary modern school in the 1950s, 'OS' on the teachers' timetable actually stood for 'odds and sods'!), but suffice it to say here that in my school class by the time I edged towards the top end of the primary school, we certainly had the full range.

Apart from a small number of children from the gentry of the big houses of the village who, I think, went to fee-paying day schools in the area – and they didn't really count anyway as living in a different world from most of us – the village school's classes contained sons and daughters of mostly farm workers, shop assistants, delivery people, a few mechanics, craftsmen, local police, and so on. In attitude terms, while most of the children saw schooling as inevitable and something to be tolerated or endured, and a few others saw it as a kind of apprenticeship to be served before you went to work and earned some money, others like myself actually simply saw it as quite a pleasant thing to do on a daily basis, without having any longer term ideas about its purpose. And as for ability, though we did not know it at the time, the range was almost exactly as I have described above – long before those terms of 'comprehensive' or 'mixed-ability' entered the educational vocabulary.

One fellow classmate I particularly recall happened also to be called David, and as his surname also began with an 'M' (he was David Manlow), and as throughout life at that school, we were always seated alphabetically in the class, he and I had adjacent desks throughout my penultimate year there. I also discovered through the register that his birthday was just two days prior to mine in October – thus he was two days older than me! However, what I have not mentioned is that David had what we would call today severe or even extreme learning difficulties. His body also seemed a little frail and he was unable to join in any robust activity; he would wander round the playground at playtime alone, lost in a world of his own. Most of all, he could not read or write at all and did not seem to be able to hold any kind of conversation with anyone. He was quite amiable and was quite simply one of those who went to school, like the rest of us. He was what he was.

I knew nothing of his home life except that he lived about a mile outside the village centre, on the opposite side from me. I also knew nothing about how he journeyed to and from school, but it says a good deal for the children and the teachers in that school that, even in those rough and ready days, he never seemed to come in for any ridicule from other pupils – despite the fact that some of them could be very cruel on occasions to their chosen targets – and neither did he ever seem to draw much impatience from the teachers. Of course, no trained teacher could have known then how to educate him in any meaningful way in that class. Thus, David sat every day, quietly and with an unsmiling but occasionally slightly puzzled look on his face, next to me. While I and others scribbled or did our sums in our exercise books or on separate sheets of paper, when we were not listening to the teacher; David had a slate and a set of chalks to 'work' with. The teacher would come to him early in the morning and afternoon and write some simple sums for him to complete on the slate, or a few capital letters for him to complete a word. She would return some time later, correct his work – if there was any to correct – say something supportive and move on. On a bad day, probably when we had provoked or irritated her, she would scold David in a mild manner for not doing anything, or doing too little or 'getting it wrong'.

But I have one reason to remember David with gratitude – he was my first ever pupil in life! Do I owe to him, I wonder, the fact that I became a teacher? It is possible.

It started one day when I saw David staring blankly at his slate and looking thoroughly miserable. I leaned over and saw on his slate where the teacher had put a few simple sums such as

CHAPTER ONE

4 + 3 =
7 + 2 =
5 - 3 =

Feeling sorry for his misery, I reached over when the teacher's back was turned and wrote a number seven after the equals sign for the top sum on his slate, and pointed at it to him. His face lit up and he looked at me quizzically. I nodded and grinned. He traced over the number seven with his own chalk. This, I realised at once, was actually a good thing because it now resembled a more shaky figure such as David himself would have written. He had now a smile on his face such as I had not seen before; whether it was for my giving him the correct answer, or because it was seen as a token of friendship, I was not sure, but I took the smile as a sign of approval. I carried on with my own work, until I saw him looking at me again and pointing to the next sum down on his list. I put my fingers to my lips to indicate silence was needed, waited until the teacher's back was again turned and wrote a number nine on his slate. This time I myself made it a little wobbly in case the teacher saw something suspicious, but in any case David went over it again, ensuring it could never be described as neat. In fact, he went over it several times, clearly enjoying himself, until it looked more like a Michelin man than a number nine. We repeated this process until all his list was complete. When the teacher came later on to look at his work, I of course made a point of being completely engrossed in my own work, ensuring in that pupil's time-honoured way that I was leaning on my elbow on my desk shielding my work with my non-writing arm, as if I did not want anyone to copy it!

'Well done, David!' she said to him and put a huge tick on his slate. 'I'll give you some more after playtime.'

So began this whole saga that lasted on and off for months. It was not continuous because David's attendance record was spasmodic and he could be away from school for a week or so at a time. Whenever he was there, sitting next to me, we played our new game. He learned that the first rule was that the teacher's back had to be towards us before we could play!

The sums got a little harder for David, of course, as the teacher seemed to think he was making progress, and he always seemed to find the subtraction answer slightly more difficult to accept and write down than addition, but mostly it went well, and David grinned more often than I or others had seen previously. In the playground, he made no movement towards me and continued to wander on his own, but there was no doubt he thought he had found an ally in me.

The writing part was more tricky than the sums, but, as it was all capital letters for David, we managed it, although I do not think he got the hang of the letters as well as he did the numbers. At one point, I thought we were nearly rumbled when the teacher commented, 'You seem to be getting them all right, David; you ARE becoming clever!' as she smiled at him. Certainly, I could see her life was a tiny bit easier because of our teamwork, but at the same time I realised that it could look suspicious, so I decided I had better deliberately give a wrong answer occasionally, just to allay any ideas the teacher might have had of a great transformation in David's brain. This, however, had its drawback! The first time the teacher put a cross against his wrong answer, David did not seem to accept it. His face was a mixture of rage and incredulity and I thought he was going to give the game away. A cross was NOT what he was accustomed to! Certainly, his belief in my infallibility must have been shattered. However, a few ticks later meant that we recovered from that potential disaster and continued, with me now ensuring that any such wrong answers were infrequent. I have to

CHAPTER ONE

confess, putting the wrong answer had briefly dented my own pride, as I rather liked the idea of infallibility! Whether this was an apparently necessary qualification for later becoming a teacher, I leave to others to judge of course!

Eventually, as a new school year dawned in the middle of one September (it was always mid-September in Kent because of the hop-picking fortnight that preceded it), I returned to my class for my final year in primary education. I sat in my usual place but – David Manlow was missing! I asked Mrs Dutton where he was and she told me, in a kindly tone, that 'David has gone to another kind of place now. He'll do very well there'.

Then, looking at me even more kindly, she said, 'I know you tried to help him a lot and it was very nice of you; but you need to concentrate more on your own work now.'

So, then it came upon me in a flash – she had known all along about my helping him! Oh, these teachers! Perhaps they were the infallible ones? Certainly, any parent of a four or five year old just starting school will recognise that belief as their child daily tells them that 'Miss X says this' or 'Mrs Y says that', firmly replacing at that time the authority of Mummy or Daddy with this new omniscience of the teacher, which lasts right through until the teacher gets them to do something they do not want to do.

That revelation of Mrs Dutton's having known all along what I had been doing also led me almost immediately to another one of even more lasting impact – the realisation that teachers are all-knowing and all-seeing. Never again would I assume there were things in school that they did not know about. It was something that stood me in good stead in my earliest days as a fledgling teacher, the realisation that my pupils had to be brought to understand that teachers really do have eyes in the back of their heads. Mrs Dutton had seen everything that David and I had been doing, even though we had carefully waited until she faced the other way!

About a year prior to that one, either because the school expanded or because the authority became more generous, the school's staff had expanded from two to three. A new teacher arrived and took what was now the middle class where I was. She may actually have been a teacher in her first year, but Miss Poole, as was her name, was certainly young. Her horn-rimmed glasses made her look rather forbidding, but she was an excellent teacher and I learned a lot in her class. The glasses, however, were her nemesis. Without them, she was near blind, it seemed, and she had a habit of regularly removing them for wiping. The class quickly found that if they called for her attention whilst the glasses were off her nose, she quite often would forget where she had momentarily placed them, and to certain pupils' amusement, she would flounder around, saying: 'Now where did I put them?' enabling several children to call out:

'Over there, Miss!'
'No, over here, Miss!'

until she became exasperated, and we knew it was time to stop. Eventually, she got the bright idea of appointing a seemingly reliable girl in the class to be her 'glasses monitor', whose job it was to at once locate the spectacles. This would have worked well, except for the fact that Brenda, the appointed monitor, had herself only moderately good eyesight. This led to the first joke, at least what I would call a proper joke, that I ever heard from a teacher to pupils. After a fairly frantic two minutes on one occasion, with both Miss Poole and Brenda confused, the glasses having been finally located, Miss Poole addressed the class:

CHAPTER ONE

'Now, I realise that you find it funny when I can't find my glasses; you think I am making a spectacle of myself!'

She paused, and waited – like any good comedian – for the jest to sink in. There was a silence. I can claim to have seen the pun, but for a second I was unsure whether laughter was an appropriate response to a teacher. I decided eventually it was what she wanted so I laughed – rather loudly and I suppose in what seemed a forced manner.

'At last! Thank you, David. At least someone has seen my pun! You are either going to be a comedian or a writer! Now, everyone, do you know what a pun is?'

Miss Poole's early forecast about my future came back to me recently as I raked over the embers of those early memories. Now I think about it, perhaps it was my first encouragement in the possibility that one might be a teacher AND have a sense of humour. Indeed, perhaps I should have taken her words as early careers advice, as it turned out to be better than any other careers guidance I ever received in secondary schooling or at university!

In the early Summer Term of that final year, we were handed some official-looking papers with 'Kent County Council' as the heading, and told that everyone had to answer the questions on them. We duly did this; they were collected in, and we got on with the important things in life – playing football and cricket, running races and scrumping.

It must have been about June that the headmistress called us all together at the beginning of the day and told us:

'You remember that you took the eleven-plus exam in April? (Ah, so that was what that was!) Well, I am pleased to tell you that two girls and one boy have passed and will be going to the grammar schools in Sittingbourne next term. The girls are Ann Linfield (she had clearly survived the air raid shelter incident fully!) and Judith Chapman.' Pause here for polite applause. She went on, 'And the boy, and he is the first boy to do this from this school is – David, David Middlewood!'

General, mostly supportive, noises followed and the day proceeded. Playtime brought a lot of questions to me from my pals, none of which I could answer. Only one or two classmates said, 'I suppose you think you're clever now, but I bet you can't–' suggesting various outrageous performances of which they were capable and some of which I had not even heard. More memorably, a girl called Margaret, whom I had unsuccessfully chased after the last time we had played a form of a chasing and kissing game under the enormous conker tree at the bottom of the playground, came up to me and whispered, 'I'll let you catch me next time!' The possibilities of being seen as intellectually able began to dawn on me at that very moment, although it was not until I was at university many years later that the issue of the extent to which brains might be some kind of aphrodisiac was debated with any seriousness!

The enormity of the impending change in my educational context only began to be realised by me when I was given a letter from the Council to take home to my parents which said, among other things, that a further letter would come from the grammar school itself very soon, detailing what was needed and so on. Only when I arrived at that new school in September did I find through chatting with new pals that those from the town primary schools, and even a few of the rural ones, had actually practised doing these exams beforehand, and also had done things in class called science and so forth. However, this exam was apparently supposed to have been about something called Intelligence Quotient (IQ) and that I must have had a reasonable amount of whatever that was!

CHAPTER ONE

Certainly, I was a good reader. As I mentioned earlier, I had been a quick and avid reader since as long as I can remember. Both my parents had left their respective schools at early ages, 13 years for my mother and 14 for my father I later discovered. Despite this, they were both perfectly literate. My father read the newspapers eagerly and also any number of old books about the army and foreign lands. My mother constantly read stories in magazines and various popular paperbacks. As soon as it was seen that I was a reader, the books began to appear. The only new ones that I ever received came from aunts and uncles at birthdays and Christmas – all the rest were second-hand. Today, I proudly own a large collection of 'old' and 'antique' books (we don't tend to call them 'second-hand' nowadays!), including some rare and valuable ones, but none is more precious to me than a few of the very earliest ones I acquired. My father's most successful part of his working life had been from the age of eighteen to mid-twenties in the regular army, and then later in the Second World War. Like so many ex-servicemen after that war, however, he was unable to find any kind of 'proper' job, and worked for about five years for the local council as a bin man, known as 'dustman' in those times. In those days, the one 'perk' of this job (no smocks, no gloves, no placing of the bins at the front of houses!) was that people threw everything out loosely – no neatly tied up bags or covers on the bins! Thus, all the goodies of odd bits of toys and knick-knacks could be had, and of course – books! So, I acquired from him all kinds of books cast out by other families. Some of these were in poor condition, but others were in a surprisingly respectable state, and some almost new, presumably unwanted gifts. Some of them I have to this day, as mentioned. Every now and then, I pick one up and re-read it – or in some cases try to re-read. In those days, books for children beyond infant age were written for what we might describe as 'mini adults', rather as forms of dress for children remained like this until about the 1950s. The vocabulary of these books is extremely difficult and, even today, I can find words in them that I hesitate to be certain of their meaning. Ones published in the nineteenth and early twentieth century are full of moralising language as well. Some of the ones I was given at birthdays are equally hard going to read and of course there were very few, if any, illustrations. However, what this meant for me then, and I only realised it much later, was that I learned to try to work out the meanings of strange words by their context, and if this was not possible, I skipped and moved on. Without giving it a thought, I realise now that I must have moved on to the second phase of my schooling with a fairly extensive home 'library' for a ten year old! My obsession with 'old books' has been with me ever since, one which I was able to indulge fully in later adult life.

So, my days of innocence were about to be over – or at least the first stages of such innocence. However, I was still to discover just how many times one has to move through innocence in life's stages before the fruits of experience could really be reaped. That was certainly true of my education, and definitely applied to an actual career in that field, as the later chapters will show.

Chapter Two

THOSE IN-BETWEEN YEARS

So my journey into the secondary stage of my schooling began one mid-September after my mother had assiduously worked her way through the list of essentials that had been sent by the grammar school. This list had not only included details of the uniform, but also how to get my bus pass and the various options for paying for my school lunches. My parents, in fact, had no option as they had no such thing as a bank account, so the concept of paying by cheque was an alien one. I therefore every Monday carried my cash in my pocket for my week's lunches, and I also now had the weirdest thing of all – a school cap! Now, not only was a uniform a strange thing – the only uniform that could identify us all from my village primary were the scabs on our knees from playground falls – but a cap! I associated wearing a cap with older men, such as my grandad, but that at least looked like a proper piece of headgear. This school cap seemed a very alien thing indeed, especially as all my friends going on the same bus to the 'modern' school in the town had no such requirement put upon them. And, in addition, in my case, a very strange thing had happened to my cap just prior to my first day at the new school.

My grandad on my mother's side was a cricket addict and followed all the news of it on the radio and in the papers, as well as having been a keen player himself. He had arranged as a family outing – a rare occurrence in itself – for us to join a coach trip in Sittingbourne to go to Canterbury to see Kent play the visiting touring side, which contained several of the 'greats' of that period. My mother and I joined my grandparents on the coach on a hot August day. We had purchased my new cap two days before and I assume I was wearing it in or something like that, since I cannot think of any other reason why I had it with me on that occasion. We boarded the coach in the town, and I was sitting next to my mother when, much to my embarrassment, a man came along the coach and said something about my wearing the cap. He said he was a teacher at the Grammar School and was I just starting next term and so on. It was very nice of him, and I remember thinking that if all the teachers were like him, it should be a great place to be going to.

It was a gloriously hot day and, although the Kent side were thrashed in the actual cricket match, the picnic food, the keeping of the score card and the sight of heroes I had only seen pictures of in the paper, made the whole thing memorable. We climbed aboard the coach for the return journey, where I sat in my seat and dreamed of emulating these titans one day. We were about half an hour from our return stop when I heard a funny noise from my mother sitting next to me. As I looked at her, her face seemed to have turned a ghastly kind of greyish white. She seemed to be pointing at my cap!

CHAPTER TWO

'Cap! Cap! Give me!' she spluttered. Mystified, I passed my cap to her. And then she, holding it to her mouth, vomited profusely into it!

'I'll get you another one,' she whispered, as her colour slowly returned. I knew my mum – she had been far too shy to ask the driver to stop because she felt sick. I felt a mixture of sorrow for her, and deep embarrassment about my cap, along with an appalling image of myself putting a cap on and its contents trickling down my face!

We arrived back, my grandparents and all the other passengers quite unaware of the mishap. As we disembarked, the kindly schoolteacher turned to me and said in a low voice:

'Hope you liked the game – but you are supposed to keep the cap on all the time, you know. Don't forget!'

Thus it was that when I arrived at the new school on my first day, I could be sure that nobody had a newer cap than myself! This was because, despite my mother's best attempts to wash and clean the cap, we both felt that the smell might linger and therefore it had to go. We could ill afford to buy another one, and I offered to wear the original one, but she would not hear of it, and a replacement new one was found two days before term began.

The other odd incident that had occurred in the summer holiday between primary and secondary school was when I awoke one Sunday morning to find a smart motor car in our garden! To be more exact, it was in the hedge of the garden, with its front against the old bullace tree that stood there. The bullace was an ancient kind of fruit which only gave us about three plum type fruits a year, but would probably now give none in the future. I found my father in conversation with someone I only knew of by reputation. He was 'Willie' March, the eldest son of the parson mentioned earlier, who was a bachelor solicitor who lived at the parsonage with a practice in the nearby town. He was a short, pot-bellied, red-faced man, known for his swagger and ebullience, and rumoured to be a fast living reprobate! He seemed to be surprisingly matey with my father on this occasion, and kept smiling at him and then at me when I arrived on the scene.

'Ah, the good lad who's going to the grammar school, I hear. Good lad! Good lad! Well done!'

I was suspicious. People like Willie March did not have anything to do with people like us. What was he up to?

'Well now, my young brother has just finished at that place where you are going. I am sure he's got some things you'd like. I'll see what he has and see if I can help. Anything I can do—'

As I listened to him and my father, it slowly dawned on me what had happened and in any case, I got the whole story later, or rather, as much of the story as my father decided to tell. Obviously with having had too much to drink, Willie had lost control of his car and ended up in our hedge (strictly speaking it was our landlord's hedge, of course, but my father was not one to let such a technicality obscure an opportunity). Desperate to avoid a scandal of the local solicitor and parish councillor being found intoxicated at the wheel, and therefore keen for no authorities to be involved, Willie was trying to persuade my father to 'keep this between ourselves'. I was confident I knew what form his persuasion had taken by the grin on my father's face and the note I could just see crumpled in his hand!

There were three specific outcomes – in addition to my father's very short-lived rise in his standard of living. The first was that a good three

CHAPTER TWO

days later, a farm tractor appeared to tow the car away somewhere (there was no garage in the village, of course); no doubt another note or two had changed hands! The second was that for several years my father seemed to retain some kind of belief that he could have access to legal advice whenever he might want it – a belief in which he was entirely mistaken, of course. The third, and the one most connected with my imminent new school life, was that my mother informed me one day in August that 'Mr March has sent you a book to help you at the grammar school. It belonged to his brother, he said'. I took the paper bag it was in, and found the book was a bible! His brother had been a fee-paying pupil at the grammar school, something which had ended with the eleven-plus system being introduced. I examined the bible, admitted that I did not possess one previously, and saw it had 'G. March' written inside the cover. I was obliged to write the appropriate thank you note, stating my appreciation and my certainty that it would be very useful to me at my new school. I had, however, no intention whatsoever of taking it with me when term began. What kind of impression would that make on any new friends! I had no wish to be known as some kind of 'bible puncher from the sticks', just as I'd read in one of the Western stories in a comic I took regularly at that time. I was relieved to think that the younger March brother had left the school, or he might have asked me whether the book was being found useful. I do not still possess that particular volume, but I happily confess to reading secretly at that time several stories of the Old Testament and finding some of the names, battles and endless 'begetting' interesting in an odd sort of way.

The next seven years of my school life were passed in this new place. I had read stories of Billy Bunter's Greyfriars, of course, and books describing life in what I imagined to be places somewhat like this, perhaps in books like 'The Fifth Form at St Dominic's', and 'Tom Brown's Schooldays', but it was not until I had been through those seven years that it dawned on me how selective state schools like mine were based on the model of those fee-paying places, fictitious and real. A school badge with a Latin motto, a school song, sports colours, House competitions – all the trimmings of public schools. To me and all the pupils, they were what they were –a whole new world that you accepted and if you fitted in, all was fine. I did seem to fit in, as it turned out, despite everything I have read since about children from working class homes feeling ill at ease in such schools. Of course I was nervous on the very first day, like any new arrival, but pretty quickly the new routine of my life became just that – the new normality. Perhaps the reasons can be shown later. There were certainly a few boys who did seem ill at ease, and each year one or two of these would mysteriously suddenly not be there at the start of a new term. Only later did I realise, through meeting one I had got to know quite well, that they had 'moved' to the secondary modern school that all my friends from the village primary now attended.

Each day of those years, I caught the bus from the village, along with these friends, travelled the four miles to town, got off first and said cheerio to them as they went on to 'the modern'. On return journeys and at weekends, we exchanged tales of teachers and rewards and punishments and escapades, and again it took me a while to realise that just as the Grammar school was aping the public school, so the secondary modern school was aping the grammar school –with its subject setting and its determination to get good examination results in academic studies! The Headteacher of their modern school, I soon discovered, had been a pupil (and school captain!) at the local grammar school, and it was only some years later that I began to work out some of the implications of this.

As for my settling in at my new school, the key here turned out to lie in the very first Wednesday afternoon games session. The teacher was the one who had been on the coach to the Canterbury cricket match and it

CHAPTER TWO

also turned out he taught woodwork and took games, and, although I did not realise it at first, he occupied the lowest rung on the hierarchical ladder of the school staff. I should have realised that when I found that he was the one who collected the dinner money every Monday morning breaktime from those who, like myself, paid weekly in cash. The 'game' on Wednesday was football, of course, and I looked at some of the other boys in their shiny new boots, socks, shirt and shorts, and nervously wondered at how brilliant they must be. My own boots were well worn, of course, my shirt as new as anyone else's, my shorts only about a year old, and so skilful had been my mother's sewing that no one could have guessed that the PE kit bag we were required to bring had been, in my case, what we call today 'recycled' from, yes, navy blue knickers! We started off a game with two makeshift teams, and from the moment we kicked off, I felt at ease. It was not just that I was reasonably good at football, but that a few of the very smartly kitted ones were hopeless! This is not a kind thing to say, because some of them were very good at other things that I was not, and of course some were very capable at playing. But the moment I found that I could outrun and dribble past several of these well kitted-out boys, I felt at home. After that, being in the form team, the house team and eventually school team meant that I had regular friends at school. These friendships were strictly for school – I never entered the house of anyone else from school for the first five years, but it was school that mattered during that period. I quickly learned to be sorry for those with little sporting prowess, knowing that my relative skill owed a lot to perhaps a matter of luck, and perhaps all that country fresh air and freedom.

I recall one boy in my form whose father it turned out actually owned a shop in town that I knew of. He became one of a group of friends for those first two years. Not that my experience of town shops was very extensive – far from it! My journeys into the junk shop next door to the one my new friend's father owned had been on embarrassing and furtive errands on behalf of my father. Dad was mad on horses, firstly because he had enrolled in the army at the age of 18 into the Royal Lancers and grew to genuinely love them, and secondly because he loved a flutter! Football pools and horse racing were his areas of expertise, so he said, although there was little tangible evidence to support any such claim. In those days, off-course betting was illegal, but everyone knew it operated unofficially with the 'agents' placing bets for their regular clients. Thus, every now and then, my father would tell me to pop into the junk shop with a folded piece of paper and give it to the man. I secretly looked at the writing once and saw it had on it something like:

'Manny franks: 1/- e/w Prince Charlie
3.00 Huntingdon'

I could decipher that the bet meant he was wagering a shilling each way on a horse called Prince Charlie at the meeting at Huntingdon, but the first two words escaped me. Later, I worked out that it was my father's code name (one of his forenames was Frank), so that the gamblers could not be identified in the event of any police 'raid'. In fact, almost certainly, the police simply turned a blind eye in those days.

The other factor that may accidentally have made me totally acceptable to the others was that I achieved notoriety by becoming the very first boy of the new intake to get a school detention! It was nothing at all heroic or particularly criminal – I had simply spoken to the boy next to me in the first History lesson; the teacher, who much later taught me History at Advanced Level, clearly had determined to impose his will from the beginning, heard me, asked my name and told me I was in Detention. This incarceration took place on a Thursday, and every Thursday morning at School Assembly, the names of the criminal detainees were read out by the Head. Thus, on the following Thursday

CHAPTER TWO

morning, my name was called out and I had to stand up in front of the whole school, along with a few other wretches. The Head even commented what a pity it was that someone in the new intake forms was 'already' in detention – in his very first week! He seemed to very clearly suggest that such people were probably marked out for a life of infamy, unless they mended their ways pretty quickly.

The actual detention was supervised by a school prefect and was an unremarkable forty five minutes after normal school time. In fact, the prefect who ran the detention seemed rather friendly towards me, chatting to me afterwards about my having an attractive sister! As a mere younger brother, the significance of that completely escaped me at the time! My more meaningful punishment came in the fact that I had been told (wrongly as it turned out) that my bus pass did not apply after the normal time, and thus I had to walk the four miles to get home! This penalty, however, was more than offset by my being surrounded by half my class on Friday morning agog to know all about 'being in detention'. I was able to reassure them about its harmlessness and perhaps I disappointed a few of them by this turning out to be my only detention of the year, a record that was quickly surpassed by several others.

One quickly got into a routine, and I learned what a timetable was and what the letters meant, which subjects were which, and which initials stood for which teacher. Not that the proper names were much used. We new boys at once became old hands and used the right nickname for the right teacher, without ever querying its origin. Thus, our form had 'Sniffer' for French, a man whom I never heard sniff once in my seven years there, 'Shagger' or 'Shaggy' for English, goodness knows why, and 'Eggo' for Maths – no idea, unless it was his baldness being suggestive of an egg? Some were just friendly, like 'Jacko' for Jackson, 'Nick' for Nicholls, and others actually by first names, like 'Jimmy' and 'Old Joe'. The head himself was always referred to as 'George'. He was a large avuncular presence and obviously never remembered my criminal start to life in his school, so I liked him for that. He did little teaching, yet I can still recall today the doggerel he taught us one day when he stood in for an absent RE teacher, and started a conversation about Latin, which, he reminded us, those that would get into the 'A' set would be studying.

'Caesar adsum iam forte
Brutus et erat.
Caesar sic in omnibus,
Brutus sic in at.'

It may well be thought that the reason I remember this so well lies in the last line! But any reader that knows no Latin has only to pronounce the above to remember it, I believe!

As for the actual learning, there was a good deal of rote learning and copying from the board. Although I like to think I have developed through life into a reasonable learner, and have even written book chapters about managing learning, I was in luck at the school because nature had given me an exceptionally good memory, a near photographic one. Words, numbers, phrases, titles, dates, and all those things came easily to me and stayed in my head. Rather like the Latin doggerel quoted earlier, I could remember long quotations and formulae after scrutinising them on the page, which of course later turned out to be a considerable asset in examinations! In later years, sharing memories with friends and colleagues about schooldays in past eras, it is remarkable how many could immediately recite certain lists that they had learned and recited from many years previously. My wife's experience of one such piece of rote learning came amusingly to light on one occasion. At the fiftieth anniversary – or thereabouts – of her

CHAPTER TWO

leaving her secondary girls' city grammar school, a group of about a dozen of her classmates of that time arranged a reunion lunch. When I went to pick her up, they told me with relish what had happened when somebody had in passing mentioned a particular geography teacher of their period at school. At the name, every single one of this dozen of these seventy year old women chanted in unison, without prompting:

'Ayrshire, Lanarkshire, Fife and Midlothian!'

The fact that these Scottish coalfields ceased long ago to exist and that knowing about them has no relevance whatsoever could not remove what they had all had religiously drilled into them! I sometimes speculate whether there is any prospect in arranging tours of places such as these for past generations of school children to revisit? After all, there must be some lists that are far more exotic than the coalfields of Scotland!

Of course, some subjects were more accessible than others to me, as indeed to other pupils. Physics and chemistry were a complete mystery to me, because no one ever explained what they had to do with the world I lived in. I assumed they only existed in the textbooks; at least in biology, I could recognise some of the plants and creatures from my village life. Music was just something to be endured by mouthing the words of some strange songs about nymphs and shepherds, or maidens in valleys, although the drunken sailor sounded good fun. English and history I loved, and I found my first forays into a new language, French, also interesting, whilst at most of maths I was competent and a positive star at mental arithmetic! At woodwork I was hopeless, despite the best efforts of that friendly games teacher, and in those lessons I laid the foundations of a life of bodgemanship which has carried me through adult life and many mishaps in several different houses, until I was sufficiently prosperous to hire someone competent to do the jobs for me. At the end of the second year, I was told I was to be in the A group and no longer needed to do woodwork. Whilst this was a huge relief to me, the fact that I was now introduced to Latin instead took me a while to adjust to. In my later adult life, I believe on more than one occasion, certain people have fervently wished that my practical skills had been better at the expense of my knowledge of Latin, which they could not quite see the relevance of! I, of course, strongly disagree. My wife Jacqui says that of course I would do so, partly because she also took Latin for a while at school, but also because she claims that my highest qualification in any case is in self-justification!

Thus, in my new school, my ability in certain favoured areas, my sporting prowess in football, hockey, athletics and cricket, and my early criminalisation meant I seemed totally accepted by the end of that first year. I had not realised of course how fit I was compared with some others. Every day running wild in the country, climbing trees, scrambling through hedges, as well as escaping at top speed from the occasional irate farmer when discovered scrumping his fruit; I even recall a shot being fired over our heads on one occasion, necessitating a very long walk home afterwards. All these had naturally toughened me and kept me in a condition which I simply took for granted. The endless conker competitions and the bruises collected through those and other such actions had also toughened my hands and feet, it seemed. However, whilst I was a very good all round athlete, I was no gymnast – I had strength and speed, but little suppleness. A further incident in PE early in the second year, to be related later, boosted my confidence and, by chance, reputation.

CHAPTER TWO

Progress - Of Sorts

Throughout my many years in schools, both as pupil and teacher, I never fathomed the nature of anyone who said they got bored during the long summer holidays. To me, and certainly all my village friends, they were bliss. The weather was fine, there was complete freedom, with endless amounts of time to spend on what one liked doing – sports or cycling or walking or just idling and reading. Who could be bored with that?

As mentioned earlier, Autumn terms began in mid-September in Kent because of the hop-picking in the first fortnight of that month. Since the age of about four, I had accompanied my mother and sister – with friends and neighbours – to the local hop gardens from about seven in the morning to about four in the afternoon. It was all playing tirelessly, until I was old enough to do some picking myself and earn some money, and I would spend the day chasing with friends around the hop gardens. New seasonal friends were made with the Londoners who came to Kent for the hop-picking fortnight as their annual holiday, and I learned cockney rhyming slang in those periods. In the September between my first and second years at the grammar school, I was haring round a corner and nearly bumped into something quite remarkable – the man coming towards me, undeniably what we knew as a tallyman (one who weighed and counted the hops in their containers), was the PE teacher at the grammar school! It had not dawned on me till that moment that those teachers existed outside of the school, let alone that one should be working here, as he clearly was! I ducked out of the way and avoided him from then on, rehearsing what I might say when I faced him. I considered various options:

'Hello, sir. I haven't got my cap on because school rules do not apply here.'

'You shouldn't be here – you're a teacher!'
'Have you come here just to spy on me?'
'Why aren't you having a proper holiday?'

All of these, of course, had to be rejected as totally inappropriate and it was not until I reflected a few years later, when I myself as a teacher sought additional income through teaching evening classes and marking exam papers, that I realised that earning some extra money in the holidays would have been his motivation. In fact, the teacher known as 'Doughnut' stayed out of my way and gave no recognition of me in that fortnight. I reflect now that I made no mention of my seeing him in those circumstances, when I returned to school, as I could not be certain whether meeting a teacher in the holidays was a matter for pride or embarrassment with my peers.

I do not think it was connected in any way, or perhaps I am naïve in thinking that, but it happened that in PE next term we were introduced to boxing as an activity. Boxing, of course, has long ceased to be acceptable in schools, but I suspect it was another hangover from imitating public schools at that time. Whatever the reason, what was it that made Doughnut select me to fight Gordon Carter in the first round of the boxing competition that we all had to take part in? Now Gordon, in the parallel class to mine, had a fearsome reputation, although looking back I realise it was based solely on his friend Terry putting it about that 'You wouldn't want to mess with him'. It could not be denied though that he was slightly taller than myself, and a good deal broader, and, most striking of all, had bright red hair!

We were scheduled for three one-minute rounds and, fortunately for me, I had already in the village had the experience of putting boxing gloves on and doing some sparring, thanks to my good friend Allen, two years older than me, who always seemed at the forefront of every

CHAPTER TWO

innovation. Gordon, on the other hand, seemed rather puzzled by the gloves, as we circled each other warily for the whole of the first round without either of us landing anything more than the kind of touch that you might apologise for if you brushed against someone by accident. In the second round, he, however, did something quite inexcusable – he tried to hit me! As I ducked under his wild swing, I threw my fist out, felt it touch something and then, off-balance, I stumbled to the floor. Highly embarrassed, I scrambled up and was told sharply by Doughnut to wipe my gloves and stand 'over there'. I looked for Gordon as I was now ready to wade in and show him my annoyance at his trying to hit me, as well as atone for my clumsiness, when I became aware that he was sitting on the floor in what appeared to be something of a daze.

'Winner is Middlewood – technical knock out!' said Doughnut, while he and another teacher and several other boys surrounded Gordon, apparently checking on his state of health.

'What's the matter with him?' I hissed to a nearby boy.
'You thumped him of course! What do you think?'

Somehow, my fist had connected with Gordon's head! He soon recovered and I now had to play the part of someone who had intended to land the killer blow all along, but who of course was at the same time magnanimous in victory. Gordon and I became reasonable friends after that, and if ever the fight was brought up in conversation, I used to say, modestly of course:

'I was just lucky!'

It was one of those occasions in life when you are actually telling the truth but no one will believe you, and you get all the more credit for being modest! Normally this works against you, but here, it suited me very well. If the match with Gordon had been a dastardly plan of the teacher which had failed, he got his revenge in the next round by matching me with a boy two years older than me who, after quickly discerning that my reputation was based on shaky foundations, gave me what is often called a 'hammering' –there were no heroics but I suffered no more than a few bruises, and perhaps a little dent in my self-pride.

Various teachers offered more opportunity than others for light relief, of course. One Maths teacher we knew as Charlie who had returned for a term from retirement, I think, had an odd speech habit of placing the stress in several words in the wrong place. So algebra became 'algeBRA' when he said it, causing us mild amusement and we tried to get him to say words that would enable us to hear him say something rude, but with only moderate success.

Another teacher, of Geography, had that particular speech defect which left him unable to pronounce the letter 'r' at the beginning of a word. When he first said, 'Wite it down', we were confused, and I like to think we did not mock him too much because he was actually a pretty good teacher. However, it was amusing to note his tactics after a short while for avoiding words which would be tricky and, as he saw it, might bring us amusement. Some names of some of the boys in the register were fated to be a nightmare to him and after one attempt to call out: 'Ridgeway, Riley and Rodwell,' he adopted a different approach. Two boys at the alphabetical end of the register were called Peter White and Andrew Wright. You can see at once the scope for mayhem in that and also the possibilities of exploitation by those two boys, both of whom I know were very capable of so doing. If I were to describe such a scene, I would have to confess it would be an invention, because Mr Ash was one step ahead of them and indeed, after that brief false start, ahead of all of us.

CHAPTER TWO

Looking at us and the register, he would simply say,

'Now, is there anyone missing today?' glaring at us even when the absence was obvious as if to dare anyone to say that 'Wiley' or 'Wodwell' or even 'Wite' was away! Those fortunate individuals were never picked on in class to answer questions for obvious reasons, whereas those with safe names like 'Middlewood' were, in my opinion, severely discriminated against.

It was a relief to me that at a certain point in my school career, I was able to drop the subjects I disliked and focus on the ones I was good at. Having got into the A class, I had been introduced to Latin which, although I did not quite understand it or its relevance, involved much rote learning which naturally suited me very well. To this day, while I understand the vocative case in Latin, and indeed found it very useful when, much later in life, I was learning grammar in my basic modern Greek adult classes, I never quite saw that occasions would arise when I would need it in talking to an inanimate object! Indeed, if I am ever found using the vocative case in addressing a door or window, apparently a perfectly sound practice in Latin, I shall know my time has come to go quietly! On the other hand, it cannot be denied that humans are known to talk very powerfully, abusively or pleadingly, to machines such as cars, washing machines and computers, especially when they let us down, but you can't expect the Romans to have anticipated everything, I suppose. On the other hand, perhaps that is exactly what they did do!

My sporting life continued to prosper, as it seemed I excelled at football and athletics in particular, representing the school at District and County levels and twice achieving national success. I was lucky to have keen support from my mother and my sister, four years older than myself, who came to watch me run in various local athletics competitions. On one occasion, when I was competing in a district championship in a half mile race (800 metres in today's terms!), I was neck and neck with a rival towards the end of the second lap. I managed to win and learned afterwards from my mother that my sister had been cheering me on most loyally and enthusiastically. It emerged, however, that she had been a little too exuberant and I found her involved in a melee with the mother of my beaten rival. Apparently, while my sister was cheering loudly, 'Come on, David!' the younger brother of my rival was shouting, not unreasonably, for him. My sister had it seems suddenly turned to him and said, 'Oh, shut up, you!' and hit him fiercely, so it was claimed, with her handbag, causing him to topple over! Today, 'Handbags at five paces' is a derogatory term for a soft dispute, but the other mother claimed that my sister's handbag must have been made of corrugated iron because her younger son would probably never recover from the blow, and be forced to live a life of permanent disability. An apology would probably have calmed it all, but my sister, who has been an amazing supporter of mine all our lives, has many qualities and one is the family trait of stubbornness. You might as well have expected her to run the race herself as apologise! The whole thing was somehow muddled through and we three left afterwards with my sister muttering darkly about the possible damage inflicted on her handbag!

As I have mentioned stubbornness as a family trait, I feel I ought to illustrate my sister's exceptionally high rating in that area through one particular educational experience. At the time of the eleven plus examination, my sister, despite her ardent desire to leave school as soon as possible, had made the mistake of doing quite well in that test, sufficient for her to be considered a possibility to go to the Girls' Technical High School in a town about twenty miles away. A letter came asking her to attend for an interview, saying that if that were satisfactory, she could be offered a place. She was furious when this letter came and insisted that in no way did she wish to go to that school.

CHAPTER TWO

My mother, not realising such interviews were optional, felt she had to attend the interview, and since it was felt I could not be left at home, the three of us set off by bus. In fact, the journey involved two buses, and for the whole of the travelling, my sister was in what can only be described as a sulk to beat all sulks. Eventually we all arrived at the school at the appointed time. My mother and sister went in, and my mother came out saying that she was to return in an hour to collect my sister after her interview. She and I passed the time at the local market and then returned to the school. We entered to be met by a stony-faced sister and an only slightly less unhappy looking teacher.

'Mrs Middlewood, I am afraid your daughter basically refused to answer any of our questions. She doesn't seem to want to speak at all!' She then added, somewhat caustically, I felt: 'And I do not think it is because she's shy! It will not be possible to offer her a place, I'm afraid.'

Well, she was certainly right about it not being caused by any shyness! My sister's mood improved considerably on the return bus journey. I suppose it could be argued that in one sense the interview had been a great success for her!

Having emerged victorious from that skirmish with the educational powers-that-be, my sister was probably convinced that the story of her defiance had been passed upwards to the Ministry of Education because the year before she was due to leave school, something she had so much looked forward to, the national government raised the school leaving age by a whole year! She was convinced it was a conspiracy against her personally, but that was one battle she could not win. When the next raising of the school age came in the early 1970s, whilst I was a teacher this time, I know there were some who felt the same as my sister had, although this event had been well prepared for this time and 'ROSLA' ('Raising of School Leaving Age') became the acronym of the decade.

As I and the others progressed through the school, the teacher-learner relationship became very slightly less master-slave, at least with those teachers whom I saw as the better ones. Looking back, I actually now believe that they were the better teachers. We all had our preferred teachers, usually based on the subjects they taught, and certainly in what became known as the 'custard wars', I was firmly on one particular side.

It happened that in my third year there, the school lunch arrangements meant that boys of my year were seen as assistants to the prefects who sat at the head of each dining table. We assistants sat at the other end and the other more junior pupils on either side. By chance, this arrangement left me the pupil of the whole lunchtime who was sitting nearest to the staff table. One day, I could not avoid hearing a dispute between Andy (the History teacher) and Davis (the chemistry one). The fact that no nickname had been invented for the chemistry master tells you that he had no affectionate place in many boys' hearts, whereas 'Andy' being a shortening of a surname indicated the opposite. As I liked History and detested Chemistry, my allegiance was easy to calculate.

It seemed that on the occasion that I overheard the dispute, Andy had inadvertently emptied the custard jug on the staff table and, when extra supplies were called for, Davis was told by the cook that there was 'no more custard'! Davis seemed adamant that Andy knew this fact and therefore should have taken less, thus ensuring there was some for himself. In fact, Davis seemed to suggest, such behaviour was typical of those with a selfish streak to their nature and thus he was not altogether surprised to hear about this aberration, knowing as he did this less admirable aspect of Andy's character. I paraphrase, of course, since the whole conversation was carried out in hissed lowered tones, which could only be picked up by my being so near and of course straining my ears for every word. So angry did Davis seem that I am sure that he would like to have thrown any custard, if he had any, in Andy's face. Andy, so it seemed to me, rather aggravated the situation by exaggerating with each mouthful just how delicious the custard was, until Davis got up and left the table with such a cluttering of cutlery and crockery that several others turned round, and were told sharply by the duty master to get on with their meals.

Such an episode was obviously worthy of passing on to friends, which I duly did after lunch, leading several of us who liked history as a subject to dub the whole thing the 'Custard Wars'. As one of my fellow historians noted, 'If you can have opium wars, you can obviously have custard wars!' and we speculated on whether there would be a peace treaty or whether hostilities would be resumed. It soon became obvious that it was to be the latter! Because of timetable requirements, the two opposing parties could not avoid being at the same lunch sitting, although I noticed that they sat as far apart as possible. Because of my prime position, I quickly became the war correspondent and was required to report most days on any latest developments. On one occasion, I was able to report that Andy, having received the custard jug first, had presented it to Davis in a manner that might be seen as provocative, assuring him that he would never dream of taking more custard than he was entitled to. Davis's response seemed to me to be somewhat cursory, although it was impossible for me to make out his exact muttered words. As the expression goes, 'if looks could kill', Andy would have been a dead man and the wars well and truly over. He survived, of course, and the next time I was able to pick anything up, he appeared to whisper something in Davis's ear as he passed behind his chair on the way to his own. Whatever he said, Davis's attempt at a contemptuous toss of the head only increased the speculation among the increasing number of Custard Wars correspondents. Many of us would have given up custard for life to have been able to see and listen to what went on between those two in the staff room, but of course that was impossible. There were, I am forced to admit, one or two misguided people who were on Davis's side. These naturally were some of those who liked chemistry, which to me at that time was merely additional evidence of their misguidedness, but correspondents are supposed to be impartial, so it is my duty to record this fact. It was very tempting after a while to invent an episode in the saga, especially one favouring Andy, and in my imagination such an episode ended with a jug on Davis's head with lumps of custard sliding down his neck! I desisted from this or any similar invention out of fear that somehow it might get back to Davis, who would probably treat my pathetic efforts in chemistry with even more disdain than he already did. Thus, I remained faithful in my reporting, and for a while an amnesty appeared to exist between the two warring factions. Clearly, antipathy between the two had existed prior to any custard disputes and I can only imagine how Davis reacted a few years later when Andy left the school, the same year that I left as a student, to take up a very senior post elsewhere, so I heard. I have speculated whether Davis's contribution to any staff leaving gift would be a) very small, b) nothing at all, c) a rather nice custard jug, or d) a packet of custard powder! I have later in my career had to give a number of farewell speeches to staff who were leaving, including a few where it was important to focus on anything but their classroom ability, but I never had the challenge or opportunity to give one on the same occasion about two members of staff who hated each other's guts!

At the age of 16 came the public examinations, called 'O' (Ordinary) Levels in those days. In fact, as mentioned earlier, I was under 16 when I sat them, because the rules about age were not nationally agreed at that time, so I went through my whole education just below the 'normal' age, entering secondary schooling just under eleven, with Advanced Levels at just under eighteen, graduating at university at just under twenty one. Many years later I placed my twin sons, James and Philip, at the opposite disadvantage by managing to have them born in the first week of September, so they were always the oldest in their year at school. Actually, research has always suggested that children born in the Autumn have the advantage anyway, and at least none of my children was born in August!

Staying On

Following reasonable success in those exams, I entered the school's sixth form and was part of a totally different world. The most important feature of this new life for all of us was that we were no longer required to wear school caps and of course we made a ritual of burning them at the end of the previous term. The school was overall strongly biased towards the sciences and maths, so that I was one of the minority of students who took at Advanced Level what were then called the 'Arts' subjects, in my case English, History, French and, additionally, Latin. I had been wrongly informed that Latin was essential for getting into University if you wanted to study English, hence I ended up studying four subjects. The classes in these subjects were tiny, four in most of them and three in Latin! By the time we actually took the exams at the end of two years, the numbers were down to ones and twos. My French teacher, known as Jimmy, was also my form tutor and wrote on my report at the end of my first year in the Sixth Form that I should 'try for Oxford'. He spoke a good deal about when he was at Oxford, primarily so it seemed because he could tell us about someone famous that he had known there – not some distinguished scholar – but Greer Garson, a very notable film star of the 1940s! I would have been much more impressed had it been someone more like Marilyn Monroe who adorned my subject folders at that time, but recognised that, even if I did go to Oxford, I was unlikely to meet Marilyn there. Oxford was soon forgotten anyway, on both sides, although it seemed to be assumed that further study of some kind was the obvious thing for me to do. My so-called 'careers' discussion had been useless, even farcical, although this was no one's fault really and led in nearly all cases of those in the 'A' group to being advised to stay on and do Advanced Levels.

That single careers session was almost exactly like the one-off session given to all students on sex education at the end of mandatory schooling. This session, as far as I recall, consisted of the deputy headmaster, a Biology teacher, showing diagrams of the different anatomies of males and females and saying hastily at the end of his brief address:

'Now, I suppose you may have questions –' (pause) 'but this is not the time for them. You can always come to my office individually if you wish, or perhaps talk with your form teacher about anything to do with this topic.'

The idea of any single boy going privately to see him or indeed a form teacher was, as he of course knew perfectly well, totally absurd. He was relieved his annual task was over and he could retreat to his office. The postscript to this story is not without interest, however. The deputy head had, it transpired, two attractive daughters and in the term before I left school altogether, I found myself suddenly promoted to being Captain of my particular House. When I asked what had happened to the erstwhile Captain, a very good pal of mine, a mumbled reply did not help. I discovered from Peter himself, however, that his disgrace was that he had been found by the Deputy in his house with his eldest daughter in a state of what may be delicately called 'undress'! Peter's account of the incident made a reference to him 'withdrawing hastily', and he was not prepared to say more! Naturally, in the school's eyes, Peter had been to blame, as the daughter was clearly a maiden of the purest reputation. Whether, the teacher's sex education sessions improved markedly after that, or whether he passed the chore to someone else, I was never to discover.

CHAPTER TWO

Moving On

At the end of that year, I had the most adult conversation that as a student I ever had with a teacher. Doughnut, whom I had got to know well through my athletic prowess, told me privately that he was leaving the school that July and would not be here in my final year. I remember feeling genuine regret at the news, especially as he told me I was to be captain of athletics next year. I was even more surprised when he went on to say that he had obtained a better job, and added:

'No more hop gardens for me!

I realised now, of course, that he had seen me in those earlier times – yet another example of a teacher being all-seeing! And he added:

'I'm going to give you a little bit of advice for your career, whatever it is.' He paused:

'Don't let the buggers grind you down!'

Then he grinned – and he was not normally one for grinning – shook my hand and left. My shock was not only that he knew and used such words, but that he had used them with me, and I was left to wonder and imagine what story lay beneath his years at that school. Had he been involved in custard wars of his own or been a victim of some kind of academic snobbery?

In my final year, I became one of the exalted group called prefects, and I recall in particular learning one valuable lesson for what was to be my future career – in teaching. Having been tormented by one boisterous thirteen year old, I hauled him before George. The Head gave him a fearsome dressing down and dismissed him from his office. To my astonishment, the moment the boy had left, George turned to me with a smile and said:

'You do know that boy will be a prefect just like you one day!' and then dismissed me. As I left, I not only reflected on the performance that George had given in front of us both, but it also flashed upon me how I had done exactly the same as that boy when I was thirteen. What a fool I was to have forgotten! I did not make that mistake when I became a headteacher myself and whenever a suitably outraged teacher would hold forth about the antics of certain youths, I confess I took a perverse pleasure in saying to them,

'Oh, yes. I remember doing that at that age. Didn't you do things like that?'

Most teachers saw the point and did remember, but there were a few who remained adamant that they never did any such thing, and I was too polite to comment about what sanctimonious little prigs they must have been, never to have misbehaved at school! Just as it seems our favourite saints are those who have been sinners, so I maintain the best teachers are those who pushed the boundaries somewhat when they were schoolchildren themselves. It is a personal theory, I hasten to add, and not one that I have researched!

One other incident should be described from my final year at school, and that is when I was involved with a much older woman! Anyone now expecting a salacious account will be disappointed, I'm afraid, but although my involvement with the opposite sex was taking up quite a bit of my life at this time, the relationship with Miss Lincoln was different. Miss Lincoln was the school secretary. She must have been about forty or fifty years old when I was seventeen, and obviously I had seen her over my years at the school. She was a fixture, just like a teacher. As a

CHAPTER TWO

prefect now, I had an occasion to go to her office on behalf of a teacher who had asked me to ask her to find something in a file. Miss Lincoln told me it would take her a few minutes to find it and I might as well sit down while she sat at her desk and searched the file. I had never sat down there before, and sank into a rather low chair so that, to avoid looking at her, which might have seemed rude, I found myself gazing at her legs beneath the desk. Now I do not think I had even noticed that someone like Miss Lincoln actually had legs, but I confess that before I had time to consider their shapeliness or otherwise, my eyes caught sight of something on her left ankle. It was a garter!

Undoubtedly, it had slipped down from its normal position to rest on her ankle. Perhaps I might not have noticed it had it not been for the fact that it was bright yellow! Canary yellow!

I was in a tricky situation. Should I ignore it? This was the obvious course, but something in me thought about the potential embarrassment for her if she got up and walked somewhere with it round her ankle – into George's room, for example! A gentleman could not allow this, so as I rose to take the paper she finally handed to me, I stammered out,

'Excuse me, Miss Lincoln, but I think your lace is undone!'

I knew it was not a shoelace but I could not bring myself to say the word 'garter'. She looked at me with surprise.

'But I'm not wearing any laces!' and looked down at her footwear as if to reassure herself that she was right. She saw and smiled, not all embarrassed.

'Oh, I see! Thank you, Middlew – David, isn't it?'

'Yes, Miss Lincoln.'

'Well, David, you are a gentleman!' Then she added, 'And probably a lady's man too, I expect!'

At which, I left her room quickly, in case she decided to replace the garter to its proper place there and then!

And so began my affair with Miss Lincoln! Well, of course that phrase would be appropriate for an English equivalent to the story of 'The Graduate' with Miss Lincoln as Mrs Robinson, although I find the line,

'It's up to you, Miss Lincoln!'

does not scan as well as Simon and Garfunkel's famous one!

What I simply mean is that for the rest of my final year, whenever our paths crossed, we looked at each other in what I became convinced was a meaningful way. She seemed to have a smile perpetually lurking at the corners of her mouth whenever we met, even in the corridor, as if we two shared some intimacy that no one else was allowed to be part of – and perhaps we did. After a while, I was suddenly seized with a striking possibility – suppose Miss Lincoln was one of those older women with a penchant for physically well-built young men of seventeen or eighteen! A further thought brought me out in a cold sweat one night – what if she invited me back to her house one day, for tea, for example? That thought cost me more than one sleepless night, while I had strange dreams about yellow garters, and I made a point of keeping well out her way for at least three weeks, only for her to say when I did happen to pass her in the corridor,

'Well, I haven't seen much of you lately!'

CHAPTER TWO

which made the whole thing much worse!

I am sure it affected my attitude towards the various girlfriends of my own age at that time, because I for a while got into the habit of wondering what they might look like when they were Miss Lincoln's age, not something recommended to go down well with any pretty 17 year old girl! I did briefly consider asking my pal, Peter, what he thought, but reckoned that he would simply recommend withdrawing hastily, so I kept my secret to myself.

In my last days at the school, exams behind me, there was fortunately no formal departure ceremony, as we just seemed to drift away from school. I was thus spared the difficulty of any formal farewell to Miss Lincoln, and looking back, I do not suppose she gave me a second thought. But to this day, I wonder what that yellow garter told the world about her – except, of course, that the world in general did not know about the garter. Just me, Miss Lincoln, and I wonder who else!

Of all the incidents described in this account of my life in education, although I can assure the reader of their truth, of only a very few do I have actual written documentation to support my version. However, I do have in a desk at home my old school reports from the Grammar school and my final report bears one comment that I cherish! As mentioned, I had a very successful school sporting life but Doughnut, who had seen me through most of it, had left with my one year to go. He was of course replaced, by a Mr Atkins, who seemed okay but in my case with limited time to get to know me. He failed to appoint me athletics captain, which of course was an initial black mark against him, but I have a lasting reason to be grateful to him. I have referred to my having both strength and speed and good eye and hand co-ordination, which meant that at almost any sport I could make at least a reasonable shot. However, supple and lithe I was not and never have been. I have never been a very good dancer, for example, although the coming of rock and roll saved me from complete ignominy. Now, one of my fellow students who did a couple of subjects with me in the Sixth Form was also a good athlete. He was not outstanding, but we were in the same relay team, for example, at county level. His name was Graham Marsh, and above all, he was superb in the gym. He excelled at forward and backward rolls, vaulting the box, walking along the beams and all those other things that require precision and balance.

When Ireceived my very last report on my last day at that school, I was able to reflect with a mostly pleasurable emotion on the teachers' comments. Mr Atkins had kindly written that I had excelled at football, hockey, athletics and listed my various achievements. He was kind enough to say that 'he should have a fine future in sport' and added that I was – 'A gifted gymnast!'

I have it in front of me, as I write! There it is in black and white. I am – or was – it seems, a gifted gymnast! If I was not revealing this now, my grandchildren in the future would have been able to say about their grandfather that he was various this and that and also– 'a gifted gymnast! Was there no end to his talents?' they might have said.

It was easy to see what had happened. Mr Atkins had mixed me up with Graham Marsh – we would have been alphabetically next to each other. Yet the other parts of my report were clearly about me. I was certainly not going back to have it corrected, and I can assure you that I have never abused that incorrect record by claiming it in any CV I have used. After all, I have never been likely to apply for any job where my giftedness in gymnastics would be a criterion for success. I would quickly have been exposed as a fraud, and no skill with words or humour would have saved me!

CHAPTER TWO

Final Stages

I gained my four subjects at Advanced Level, three at modest or medium grades and the Latin with what is known as a 'scrape', and entered upon another long summer break without knowledge of what might follow. I had applied to a university but had heard nothing. July and August that year were spent in harvesting and fruit-picking, and September came and almost went, until one day, the sister of my good friend Doug (she worked in the village Post Office), appeared running towards me in the orchard. There was a telegram for me! This was an event indeed, not just me for but for the village because telegrams were rare things. The contents told me to attend for an interview at the University in Reading in three days' time!

I travelled there by train and emerging in a town that I knew nothing of except that it was the home of a famous biscuit manufacturer, I caught a bus to the university in old redbrick buildings and reported to the actual Professor of English himself. It was not really an interview because it was clear that a place had now been reserved for me. The professor explained that a student who had been expected had dropped out and they needed a male to replace him. I think he said that if I had been a girl, I would not have been there or some such thing. Thus, I went home, reported my fate and, having missed Freshers Week, joined the English BA Honours course. That professor was not famed for his academic prowess, it seems, and the only reference I have ever found to him was in Margaret Drabble's book on Angus Wilson, where he is described as a manic depressive and a repressed homosexual. He was, however, a fine lecturer on his favoured subjects of Austen, Dickens and Yeats, for example.

My three years there, in a new building by then, brought me huge insights into the literature that I had loved since primary school, and generally I thrived. There are few tales of humour to recount from that time because university humour always seemed rather contrived to me – you saved it all up and did slapstick things during Rag Week. Everyone to their taste and they say that humour is an individual thing after all. This is not to say that I did not have a lot of fun and enjoyment at university because I did, but as it mainly involved either relationships with female students or humorous literature, it is not really relevant here. So, passing over my breaking my leg in playing football for the university first team (bringing my sporting career to an early end) and shaking hands with the widow of the great poet W.B. Yeats as being my two most memorable moments, I can say that I received my degree scroll showing that I had achieved a good degree and was ready to begin training for my next step. I had definitely decided to become a teacher and find out what it was like on the other side of the desk!

PART B
THE OTHER SIDE OF THE DESK

Chapter Three
FIRST STEPS

Getting Ready

Having decided I wanted to be a teacher, the first question to be settled was where I should do my one-year post-graduate training course. Eventually, I decided to do this at the same university where I had taken my degree in English. This decision had also been confirmed by the fact that my applications to two other places had been rejected! In the course of this account of my career, I have made sure to mention – and will continue to do so – the setbacks and rejections as well as acceptances and successes. It is interesting to speculate how many of our CVs might look so very different if we had to include all our rejections as well as our successes. I know of one ex-colleague who gained his school headship eventually, after 22 interviews and more than 70 applications! But all any prospective employer knows is that you are applying at their particular school, not that you have been

CHAPTER THREE

rejected by countless others. We are told that we learn through failure, I suppose, and there is no evidence as far as I know that someone who gets the job after twenty attempts is any better or worse than someone who hits the spot first time. You can argue that I would say that anyway, I suppose!

Anyway, as part of my training year to gain my teacher's certificate (PGCE) and indeed a Post-Graduate Diploma in Education, I was told I was expected to spend two weeks 'observing' in a primary school. It seemed the obvious thing to do to choose my own village local school that I had attended long ago, and described earlier, and so I arranged to turn up there in the relevant July. It was an odd time to be there because it was at the end of the summer term, and there appeared to be very little actual schoolwork going on. Mrs Dutton had long retired, of course, and the headteacher was a jovial man, pleased to see me, and even more so when he heard that I liked sport. He was keen on cricket; it was summer, and what I most remember is how the daily timetable there was firmly constructed around that game.

At morning break, virtually everyone was enlisted, boys and girls, in a game in the playground, and the summons to end the break and return to lessons at the specified time was indicated by a hand bell being rung by a monitor at a signal from the head. There was a logic to this, I soon discovered, and that was particularly apparent when the Head was batting! If he were still batting when the appointed time came, no signal was given, no bell came and morning break continued until he was either out, became too tired to continue, or reached a particular score that satisfied him. On one memorable occasion, he was obviously in good form and his score moved relentlessly towards fifty! When he reached forty or thereabouts, I believe he glanced at his watch, saw it was way past the normal time for lessons to resume, and I could almost see him calculating that in the grand scheme of things, what might a few minutes fewer of mathematics or geography matter compared with the epoch-making event of the school's leader reaching a score of fifty? And who can say which indeed was the more important? Of course, I believe one or two of the older boys were canny enough to realise that if they sent him down some easy bowling to ensure he stayed in, his score would grow and lessons would be deferred, but my suspicion was impossible to prove. As he reached his target with a glorious cover drive past the playground's conker tree boundary, he shouldered his bat, magnanimously declared time was up and signalled for the bell to sound. I noted that the applause from the pupils was accompanied by some furtive grins and as I looked at my watch and found that it was now only 20 minutes until lunch break, I realised why! Still, everyone seemed quite happy about the situation, and after all, I was only an observer!

It had been strange to see some of the pupils' names on the school roll and realise that some of them were the children of the very people who had been my own classmates all those years earlier. A small but regular number of boys nowadays passed through to attend the Grammar school in town, so it was no longer the novelty it had been in my long ago era. Already I was part of history, and I was made to feel even more so nearly a decade later when I was invited to attend part of that school's centenary celebrations. When they reached their one hundred and fiftieth recently, I am sure they quite reasonably assumed that I was beyond even history, and had probably gone to be ticked off in that great register in the sky!

When the post-graduate university term began in late September, I joined the 80 or so other post-graduate students for lectures and seminars on various educational topics and for some teaching practices in local schools. The lectures were very unmemorable, except for the ones on child psychology, and the main pleasure came through new friendships. By chance I met another post-graduate who had been to the same grammar school as myself; I vaguely remembered Arthur as someone two years ahead of me at school, but he, a new friend, Derek, and I hung around together at coffee breaks and during the evenings, often complaining, as many others did, about being treated 'like children' instead of the seasoned adults that we felt we were. I cannot recall the details, but virtually the whole group became so fed up that it was proposed that a petition demanding a more adult approach in the whole course be sent to the main culprit, the Professor of Education who was the Head of the Department. Two energetic female students drew up the petition with a wording that we all agreed on. We also agreed it was from all of us 'equally', as we all felt the same. One of the young women said:

'Right! Now we all need to sign our names. Who's going first?'

I, like everyone else, had rather assumed she would but it appeared she and her friend felt they had done the wording and that was sufficient. I found myself with a biro in my hand and saying,

'Oh, I'll start' and duly signed my name, followed by Arthur, Derek and everyone else. The petition was then delivered to the professor's office, and we awaited a response. He arrived at his normal time a few days later, delivered his lecture, finished ten minutes early and pronounced that he would respond to 'a certain document he had received'. Again, I do not recall the gist of his response except that we found it boring, pompous and evasive, focusing on our need to behave as 'professionals'. He then turned his special ire on what he termed the 'ringleaders' of this escapade, and he glanced at the list of signatures, my name by chance being at the top of course.

'Mr David Middlewood, for example, needs to remember he is supposed to be becoming a member of a noble profession which stands for discipline, authority and order, and he and some others should be embodying these things, rather than fomenting the opposites!'

That was me, apparently! I looked around but the two young women who had devised the petition were assiduously gazing at the floor, and Arthur and Derek were greatly amused at the whole thing. I opened my mouth, thought better of it, and the whole thing just faded away. However, we noticed that things did improve markedly, so perhaps the Professor was employing a tactic well known in some dubious circles for dealing with a complaint. This tactic involves denying the causes for the complaint completely, but altering things anyway, pretending that nothing has happened, so as to give no further cause for such a complaint. Later on, it may even be possible to take credit for the changes! In fairness to that Professor, although my heart sank when I learned that he was personally coming to observe me during my long whole term's teaching practice, I have to say that he was in fact very fair, gave me some useful tips and passed me through well at the year's end.

On one of my teaching practice placements that lasted a fortnight in a local co-ed secondary modern school, I did a mixture of observation, and teaching a few selected lessons. For a reason never explained, the mixed classes were divided occasionally for a few lessons according to gender and I was given on one day a class of 13 year old boys to teach 'Huckleberry Finn', and on another a class of girls of the same age to do 'A Midsummer Night's Dream'. These had the advantage of being small in number, about 14 in the group, but the choice of material was not what I would necessarily have selected. The girls' class in particular was not an immediate success. As we tried to read the text, one of the girls insisted that her character was called 'Hernia' (instead of Hermia!) and every time the name came up, the girls went off into peals of

CHAPTER THREE

laughter. Now the play IS a comedy, and laughter is thus a good thing, but as anyone with knowledge of 13 year old girls will know, when the laughing becomes giggling, it is usually highly contagious. Very soon, virtually all the class was giggling non-stop, and, possibly my being a young male in his early twenties merely adding to the context, I was in despair. Strict instructions and pleadings were equally ineffective on my part, and I was praying that no one would enter the room. Eventually, I cried, 'Listen!' pretending to be doing that very thing by cupping my hand over one ear. They did halt giggling in a stifled sort of way, and I said, hardly knowing what to do,

'I need to tell you a joke!'

That did get their attention and distracted them from Shakespeare's forest for a moment. I had not even got a joke prepared!

'There was a young lady called Hermia,' I blurted out.

They were all listening now!

'Who had a most painful hernia,' I added.

Hoots of laughter now! I had their attention.

'Now,' I said, 'do you know what a limerick is?'

Some did and some did not. I explained the structure and quoted an Edward Lear example. Their giggling had now at least turned to smiling and chuckling. Then came the feared question:

'But, sir, what can rhyme with Hermia and Hernia?'

I think this was perhaps where my ability in much later life to entertain the residents of a nursing home through my limericks must have been born. I thought quickly:

'Turn yer'? 'Burn yer?' Even 'Vernier?' Not really.

Then it clicked and I triumphantly said:

'But when she got kissed,

The pain went in a mist,

Thanks to that boy from Hibernia.'

Well, although they had not much, if any, idea about where or what was Hibernia, they all laughed and I do mean laughed and not giggled. After explaining Hibernia, I was able to talk about limericks as an example of a simple poetic structure, and amazingly the rest of what had now become a poetry lesson passed off well enough. As mentioned earlier, I have had many reasons to admire Shakespeare but just at this moment I wished that he had had the imagination to have produced a book of limericks as well as all those wonderful sonnets; the lesson then would have been an even greater success. What the teacher who had to follow me and resume with the actual play made of it in the next lesson, I have no idea!

When the second term came and it was time for me to spend the whole of it as a student teacher in a Kent school about 30 miles from my home, I decided to invest in my own vehicle to get to the school. This vehicle was a small motorcycle and although I had not ridden one before, I got my provisional licence and learner plates and started practising via a few local trips out. Early in this period, I was showing the motorcycle to a couple of my friends, Allen, he of the boxing gloves, and John, my next door neighbour, when, as ever, my father joined us, and I soon heard the expected words:

'Ah, I know these. I had one just like it once!'

This was very unlikely to be true, I knew, but Allen and John were duly impressed.

'Give me a kick start, and I'll have a run on it.'

These were my father's next words and, with a sense of foreboding, I assented. I should explain that my father had long had a very rheumatically painful right leg and walked with a stick, although he was able to cycle reasonably well. It was necessary, therefore, for someone to kick start the machine for him. We did so, the engine puttered into life, my father sat astride and off he went 'up the lane' as we called it. We lived well outside the village and the next village was about four or five miles away with two very steep hills en route. We waited for him to return, as we stood outside home. And waited – and waited – and waited! Nearly half an hour had elapsed before we had to recognise that all was not well, so we got our bicycles and set off the way he had gone.

We found him eventually at the bottom of the first of those two hills, sitting disconsolately in the hedge. He and the motorcycle were both apparently unharmed, but what he had had was time to get a story ready.

'I think it's run out of petrol.' I checked – it had not!

'The steering is a bit wobbly.' It wasn't!

'The brakes are quite sharp.' They were!

It became clear to us that he simply had not known how to either stop the vehicle or turn it around to come back, and felt that toppling gently over into a hedge might be the least painful option. We hauled him and the bike up the hill and made a very slow return home. I could only hope that Allen and John would not be so ready to believe my father's tales of his prowess in future.

The motorcycle managed to get me halfway to the school where I was doing my practice, where I stored it and got a lift from another teacher from the school for the rest of the distance in his somewhat rundown car. We always seemed to arrive on time, and my term there was enjoyable. As mentioned, even when the Professor visited me to observe my teaching, he was not displeased, and even though his ideas on teaching poetry were very different from mine, I kept my counsel because I calculated that if I dissented too much, he might recall my status as the putative leader of a rebellion, something he had clearly now forgotten! I certainly did not consider limericks as an option for my lesson which he observed!

First Realities

At the end of my training year, I had with all the others to sit the exams for the official teacher's Certificate and Diploma. It did not seem possible to treat these exams as seriously as the finals I had taken for my degree, but passing them was necessary. We had been obliged to opt for a subject outside of our normal studies, presumably to make us a more 'rounded' person. I had put down Music as mine because there was a very attractive young woman who was keen on that, and it seemed an opportunity to get to know her better. It turned out that all those who had opted for Music had to sing in a choir! The lecturer in charge found he had over 50 people to organise and, instead of individual auditions, he asked the men to just stand in the appropriate group. I stood with a group of about seven whom he started calling tenors, and seemed pleased he had as many as that! I recalled my mouthing music lessons from early Grammar school days and stood with the rest mouthing various words while they sang heartily. There was little chance of being found out with that number of singers, but I did not fancy spending too much time opening my mouth with nothing of any worth emerging – if I had wanted that, I told myself, I could have become a politician. Thus, after two sessions, I truanted and, apparently, no one noticed – except the attractive young lady who decided I was not what I seemed. Such a relationship clearly would have been doomed anyway. What chance have you got when someone finds out the truth about you so early on?

For the exam, we had also to study a 'person of importance in the history of education' from a specified list, which included among others, I remember, Montessori, and Saint Ignatius of Loyola. I ticked the latter, but actually forgot later which person I had ticked. My reading during that year was focussed on poets and novelists that my English degree syllabus had not included and I had become fascinated by William Golding, Rosamond Lehmann, John Osborne and Emily Dickinson among others. When the day came for the exams, one paper included a question along the lines of 'Write about your chosen person of importance, stating their significance and what you feel you have learned from them'. Of course, I was stumped, as I knew nothing, not even who was my choice. Given that it was only one question out of five, I calculated – or perhaps gambled – that a solid nought for that answer might still give me enough to pass. I decided that I would at least be honest. I do not remember my exact words, of course, but they were along the lines of the following:

'All the people on the given list were of course very important, but education would have survived and progressed without any single one of them. Without the important person I have chosen as my special study, education and teaching could not exist. I refer of course to – the child! After all, teachers only exist because children need to learn, just as we teachers did when we were children. The first thing to note about a teacher and in deciding whether he or she will be a good teacher is, I believe, whether they actually like children. I for one am passionate about my subject, which happens to be English, but if I see it as being more important than the child or young person who will benefit from it, I may become an efficient instructor but never a good teacher. If I am fond of children and young people in general, then teaching my favourite activity to people I like can only be a pleasure; if there are individuals whom I like less than others, then the challenge is simply greater.'

And so on. I suppose I was setting out my philosophy and I thoroughly enjoyed the 40 minutes or so I spent on that answer, as I became absorbed and the time swept by. When the results were given out, I was awarded my Certificate and also my Diploma – with a credit! My mark for that paper was my highest of all. Nothing was said about my irrelevant answer, but I felt vindicated. As I reflected, however, I wondered whether the lesson I had learned was about how to flannel through something without any real knowledge of it, or about being honest and true to oneself, or perhaps a bit of both! It is certainly true that of all the very poor teachers in my career that I met, and thankfully that was a small number, what virtually all of them had in common was that they did not like children! Why they were in teaching was a mystery – but that perhaps is another story.

CHAPTER THREE

Starting in reality

At the end of the training year, I had, of course, to apply for actual teaching jobs, and after a few ignored applications and one failed interview, I obtained a post at a grammar school in an Outer London Borough on the south side of the city. The principal made it clear at my interview that he thought my spoken accent somewhat less refined than he would have wished, but, as I had a very good degree, I could have the job! I managed to stay there two years, teaching English with a tiny amount of History and French. I also naturally did one games session per week. I say 'naturally' because it seemed that any young and fit teacher was regarded as capable of 'doing' games lessons. As a footballer teaching the boys in a rugby-playing school, I initially felt some anxiety because of my very shaky grasp of the rules of the latter. However, the pupils I was given were 11 year old boys in their first year and as long as I shouted out 'Well done!' and 'Bad luck!' occasionally, as well as proudly blowing the whistle when they passed the ball forward (that rule I did know!), everyone seemed happy enough. Their questions about which team I played for as an adult I simply replied to by mentioning a professional football club where I had had a trial just before my leg was broken, and they seemed satisfied with that for some reason. I received a letter from the Borough Authority at the end of that year, saying I had successfully passed my teacher probation period and I was now a 'proper' teacher!

It was the only job in my whole teaching career that I did not much enjoy, so I was pleased when at the start of my third year I saw a post advertised for an English teacher (with a very small extra amount of money as well!) at a school in the Medway towns, only a few miles from where I was then living. My head of department at my first school was at that time a man well-known in the English teaching world – he co-edited a journal for English teachers and had also published two children's books. He had not been involved in my selection and had never been to see me in my classroom. I asked him if he would supply me with a reference in my quest for this new post and he replied:

'Yes, of course. Jot something down yourself and I'll sign it!'

I wrote a factually accurate statement about what I had done in my two years there, he signed it and I took it to the successful interview for what turned out to be my next post. As disappointing and disillusioning as my first two years had been, so my next four years in this post were delightful and also as professionally rewarding as I could have wished. My new Head of Department was one of the nicest people I have ever known and the headteacher, although I saw relatively little of him, turned out to be a wise and very astute person.

Altogether, of course, my first few years in the teaching profession, as with anyone beginning a career, were all about learning what may be called the 'tricks of the trade', and shedding the naivety with which so many young entrants to the profession began in those days. I personally believe that teaching is ultimately a matter of performance and the teacher therefore is by nature some kind of performer. After all, how can you have a job which involves standing in front of and mingling with about thirty children or young people and NOT be a performer? Of course, the phrase 'teacher performance' has in recent decades taken on a quite different meaning, that of achieving certain outcomes, especially in exams or tests, and I myself have written about that aspect, deploring like many others the excessive focus on those outcomes. If you think about the best teachers you have had, I can almost guarantee there was something of the performer in each one of them. You can compare it to acting very readily. When you enter a classroom, you take on a persona, just as actors do on stage, and like most great actors you absorb yourself in the part whilst at the same time being yourself. This

CHAPTER THREE

is why many good actors bring different interpretations to the identical role of the same character. A good teacher does not 'put on' an act, but instinctively becomes the teacher while being true to themselves. Sam Mendes, the famous theatre and film director, described how the really great actors 'understood how to take the work seriously, but never yourself'. I can think of a few school leaders who took themselves too seriously in believing that it was their personality that gave them their authority, instead of understanding that it came from the role they held. The effective ones were those who understood that, and then had a personality in themselves that commanded respect and even liking. These 'tricks of the trade' to be learned in early teaching days, therefore, were about finding those things to do that fitted with your own personality and character and would therefore work for you.

One aspect of that youthful naivety that new teachers might begin with, and certainly did in days gone by, is believing that everything would turn out alright just because you wanted it to. My wife Jacqui recalls how in her first year as a primary school teacher, working in a Midlands city with children from deprived backgrounds, she wanted them to feel the forces of nature and the freedom from their cramped conditions. She got permission to take her whole class of five year olds to a large public park, and foolishly ignored the advice of another teacher to take a whistle with her. She recalls how she took them to the top of a rise in the green park, and, raising her arms in the air, cried out:

'Now, just run!'

And they did – every single one of them! Within a minute, she realised in a state of sheer panic that there was not a single one of them to be seen. They had all gone – disappeared. Her whole future teaching career flashed before her – or rather the lack of a career, any career at all in fact. Desperately, she started hunting and it took over 90 minutes to round them all up. People, kindly strangers, would come up to her holding a small child by the hand saying,

'Is this one of yours?'

and at least two grandmothers brought their own grandchild to her, saying that they thought they were supposed to be at school that day! She thinks with horror of the consequences of such an action in later decades, but can laugh at her own folly in those innocent times!

Whilst school outings are well known as the teacher's nightmare if the numbers do not add up when preparing for return, my own experience was rather different at my second school, when, on one memorable occasion, I managed to come back with MORE than I started out with! It happened like this.

The ancient eighteenth century school building in the city centre in the Medway town was being replaced with a brand new building outside the city, with green fields all around. Whilst I was there, the school was therefore on two sites. Like all staff, I spent some teaching time in this new place, and all the sports fields were there anyway. Next door to these playing fields was the village of Borstal. The name 'Borstal' was for many generations in the United Kingdom synonymous with a type of institution for young offenders, because the first of these institutions was actually in that village, and was so at the time I was there. Part of that particular Borstal's grounds included a farm where the young male inmates worked for part of their sentenced time there. Like all young teachers, and as at my first school, I did games as a small part of my timetable, mostly hockey and athletics this time, but also the traditional cross country – essentially a winter activity. I remembered it only too well from my own school days as, apart from gymnastics, it was the only sporting activity I did not much care for. Apart from

CHAPTER THREE

the odd masochist, who could actually LIKE cross country, we used to say? However, as a young teacher, for a few weeks each year, I dutifully put on my tracksuit and with a couple of other staff led or followed – in my case mostly followed – the large group of pupils round the course, our job being to chase and chivvy any slackers and exhort them on to the end. There were usually two or even three classes together, so, allowing for the bearers of sickness notes and absentees, upwards of 60 or 70 trudging and reluctant youngsters were on the journey. The other job of a teacher would be to check on skivers, which was done by counting the runners at the halfway point to ensure that no one had fled or taken an illegal short cut. On one occasion, I was on this particular duty and dutifully counting them through, the official number having been given to me as sixty-two. I counted them through:

'Fifty-nine. Sixty. Sixty-one. Sixty-two. Sixty-three. Sixty-four.'

Wait a minute! That was too many! I actually ran hard myself then, taking an illegal short cut and reached the point where the course emerged on to a main road before curving back to school.

'Too many! We've got too many!' I panted to the PE teacher in charge there.

He raised an eyebrow:

'Damn!' he said. 'I bet they've done it again. Probably on a blasted bus by now!'

He explained to me that on a couple of previous occasions, whilst our runners were passing though the farm, one of the Borstal inmates working on the farm, having prepared beforehand with vest and shorts underneath overalls, had slipped off the outer clothes and simply mingled in with our group, picking a place where the numbers were most crowded. Most of our runners were too tired to notice and possibly didn't know every other person anyway. The newcomers passed through the farm's exit with no trouble, boarded a bus on the main road and thus made their bid for freedom!

'Of course, they don't get very far. Usually out for about two hours, I should think. Still, I suppose they must think it's worth it?'
'What happens to them when they're caught?'
'Oh, a month or so added to their time, I think.'

I think it happened twice in my four years there, and deep down, I suspect that both teachers and our runners possibly hoped that one day someone would really escape 'properly', make the headlines and we could all brag a little about knowing how it was all done. So that was my special outing experience, and at every school trip I have been on since, I have thought of those extra lads when I am checking my numbers for a return journey.

I have never again acquired any extra personnel on a school venture, except on one occasion when I took a party of Advanced Level English students to see a production of Christopher Marlowe's 'Edward the Second'. We were just preparing for our coach to depart when a member of the cast rushed up to it, asked which way we were heading and then begged a lift to drop him off near his home. This was right on our route and we were slightly flattered to have him, even though he had played a minor character, in fact several minor characters, including being one of the murderers. If you know the gruesome way in which Edward met his death, you will need no description, but suffice it to say it had involved a red hot poker pushed up where it could hurt most. Some of the female students had found the ending gruesome indeed and regarded the passenger suspiciously, as if they were not quite ready to distinguish theatre from reality. A few boys, however, could not resist calling out regularly to him, 'Bottoms up!'. He took this all in good spirits and when he departed from the coach, he pretended to walk like someone who had indeed been injured thus! Instead of an insightful analysis of the play on the coach going home, the discussion was inevitably all about gruesome tortures!

Another duty assigned on occasions to more junior staff on those cross-country duties was that of vetting the various notes excusing the holders from that particular exercise. I was shown the ropes first by the Head of PE, a long-serving veteran on the staff, who ran his department like the traditional sergeant major.

'Now first. Having no kit! All rubbish! Never accept that. We keep loads of spares here, so whatever they claim to not have, just give them one from the pile.'
'What if it doesn't fit?'
'All the better! If they're uncomfortable or look ridiculous, they won't forget again! In fact, if you can pick out and give them vest or shorts that look stupid, so much the better!'

There was, I had to admit, a kind of rough justice in that. When I saw someone running slowly in the odd style of only swinging one arm instead of both, I knew it was because they were using the other arm to desperately hold up a pair of shorts several sizes too big for them!

'Now, others. Look at this one: "Johnny is having trouble with his feet again".'
'Of course he is – he's having flaming trouble putting one of them in front of the other. Lazy–! Ignore that. He can run – even walk if he wants to – but he goes!'

'Here's another. "William finds breathing difficult." Of course he does! He finds everything difficult – especially living! He can go – as slow as he likes, but he goes.

'Look at this one. "James has only just recovered from illness, having been away from school for a week. I think he is not ready to do any strenuous exercise yet." I bet he's not. It will do him a power of good to be in the fresh air! Send him round, and tell him to gulp in that air when he's going!'

I began to see how the Head of PE operated; he had an almost divine belief in the power and goodness of physical exercise and thought that all attempts to wriggle out of such an activity were the work of the devil! When an absolutely cast iron excuse was provided, such as a leg in plaster after a broken ankle, you could almost sense the repressed fury and frustration of the man, and the poor innocent was set on to carry out some menial task, which the Head of PE clearly thought would deter them from ever again doing anything so stupid as breaking a limb. One felt he longed to accuse the culprit of deliberately breaking it in the first place! UNLESS, and I noted this, if you had been injured playing for the school first rugby team; then it was a different story.

'How are you, Wilson. Hope the arm is improving? You'll be okay soon, you know! Mind you be careful!'

I never heard of any parents complaining about this harsh treatment of their offspring; perhaps he was as tough with the parents as with their children; perhaps they simply did not dare to? I sometimes wanted to ask him what he would say if a parent reported that her beloved child had 'had the runs', but I never dared to either ask or suggest a possible answer!

CHAPTER THREE

Strategies

These earlier years, as well as developing subject knowledge and all the professional acumen necessary for an effective career in teaching, are also about developing strategies through experience for managing as many challenging situations as possible. I had already seen through my experiences that young people do not respond to shouting or ranting, but I found they have an innate sense of fair play, and although you, as the teacher, are ultimately in control, this is something that, although you cannot appeal to it perhaps, you can certainly utilise it.

It can be difficult to use the right word sometimes in describing these strategies. What is one person's 'bribe' is another person's 'pact'. For example, my lifelong friend, Doug, earned some money as an 'Unqualified Teacher' at the age of about eighteen before going up to university. He was inevitably given the worst behaved class, and chaos was expected to ensue. Some of the teachers were amazed how orderly the class was while Doug was with them, when they themselves had struggled. What they did not know was the he had 'negotiated with' or 'bribed' them that, if they behaved themselves, he would stay after school and arrange playing football with them every single day'! As he loved football, it was no hardship for Doug, so everyone was content perhaps.

It was, of course, normal practice for younger and most inexperienced teachers to be given some of the least easy classes, as happened with Doug, and where classes were set or streamed, this often meant the least able groups. It happened that, although my school timetable was perfectly fair, I was asked one day by my Head of Department if I would do him a favour, which turned out to be a real baptism with a 'tricky' class. The school had been asked by a local Further Education (FE) College if they could provide, in an emergency that had occurred, an

English Teacher to teach a group of 16 year olds on a Friday afternoon from three to six o'clock. If I agreed, I would be released early from my own school, and I happened to have a 'free period' then anyway. Moreover, I would be paid extra for this one class. I could refuse nothing to Brian, my Head of Department, and I reasoned the extra money would be very welcome, and as it was only for half a term, about six weeks, I agreed. Of course, as Brian pointed out, it would mess up my 'poet's day', but the money would compensate. This allusion to 'Poet's Day' will at once be familiar to teachers all over the English-speaking world, as not referring to a day for becoming immersed in Eliot, Yeats, Wordsworth, Emily Dickinson or any other bards. I had discovered at this school that it was equally used by scientists and mathematicians to describe Friday, it being an acronym for 'P---- Off Early, Tomorrow's Saturday!' Every school I subsequently worked at was familiar with that acronym, whilst the thousands of other such acronyms beloved by government departments and forwarded to teachers could be easily forgotten!

I did not know at that time a great deal about FE colleges, but managed to have a preliminary meeting with someone from the place who was Head of General Studies. She informed me that my class was a group of building apprentices, adding:

'And I think it is only fair to tell you that they are not keen on English Studies – or anything else come to that – especially on a Friday afternoon. They are more interested in the two days following! You can teach whatever you like though. I'll just leave you to it.'

With those encouraging words, I was left to ponder the wisdom of my agreeing to take on this new challenge. I realised later how much of an understatement 'not keen' was.

CHAPTER THREE

I arrived on that first Friday afternoon and managed to reach the correct room where about a dozen youths (all male in those days as females in the building trade were unknown then) were chatting in groups, bodies sprawled across the desks. I recalled one piece of advice I had been given that, if faced with an apparently hostile group, find the leader! Actually, the leader found me – and pretty quickly too. A large burly youth eyed me up and down, before saying:

'Are you Mr Middlewood? That's a funny name!'

I heard myself saying,

'No, my name's Muggins, because I've got you lot on a Friday and in the afternoon!'

There was a slight pause then Gary, the burly questioner, burst out laughing and all the others followed suit. That settled things for at least a while and, after an introduction which they at least pretended to listen to, I put them into two or three small groups to discuss a topic. As I moved around, it was painfully obvious that Gary's group for one was way off task in talking about my prescribed topic and seemed to be discussing various gambling strategies.

Having some slight knowledge of the topic, thanks to my father's wayward past, but lacking technical detail, I dived in:

'What's a triple accumulator then?' I asked him.
'You don't know what a triple accumulator is?' he said scornfully.
'No. Is it a literal or a figurative expression?' I asked.
'What's a figurative thingy?'

This was my chance!

'I'll tell you what. You explain to me and everyone else what a triple accumulator is, and we'll all listen and discuss. Then, I'll explain what a figurative expression is and you all have to listen and discuss. Is it a deal?'

Gary, like any sensible negotiator, carefully weighed up the pros and cons of my offer and then he accepted, and so began a six-week period of debate which I can honestly say was both enjoyable and, I like to think, profitable on both sides. I myself learned about some topics, in addition to the technicalities of gambling, that would not be on any official school syllabus, although there were a few – mostly indecent – themes that I did have to veto! Gary and the others read some things they would never have tried without my agreed pact with them, and I am confident that their debating skills were enhanced. They seemed genuinely sorry to see me go at the end of that term, although I do not deceive myself that I quickly became anything but a distant memory in their hectic lives. Although I had learned what a triple accumulator was, I have never been enough of a betting person to take advantage of Gary's tuition.

Having become aware of teachers knowing so much more than I, as a pupil, had realised, it was important in those earlier years that I knew how to promote in my pupils' consciousness the notion that I too was all knowing and all seeing – not about the subject or topic, but about what they were doing in class! Some of it was relatively easy. If, for example, while turning to a board, you caught sight out of the corner of your eye someone in the back row passing something to another student, you did not swing round triumphantly as if catching them in the act. All that did was teach them to be more effectively furtive next time. What you did, of course, was to continue looking at the board and simply comment such as:

CHAPTER THREE

'I should stop doing that, Trevor. Either you'll get into trouble or you'll have to give it to me anyway at the end of the lesson!'

This produced the right amount of bewilderment as to how you knew and a more considered risk assessment of the perils of doing it again. On one occasion I saw A copying from B, with B showing off by knowing the right answers. My response was to say to B.

'I am sorry to find you copying from A! I shall have to penalise you for it, of course, in the marking.'

B's mouth opened to protest his innocence, and, realising the consequences of betraying A, simply agreed and did not allow the copying again – to the benefit of both A and B.

One practical advantage I had in my second post was that it occurred during the 'Great Freeze' of the 1960s, as it was known. Being in a very old building with great furnaces in some rooms, which had to be regularly topped up via scuttles of coal, most lessons had to begin with warming up exercises, pupils were allowed to wear gloves and scarves in class for the coldest period, and therefore there was a general spirit of 'we are all this together', and the mood was decidedly positive. Even the River Medway was frozen over for the first time in more than a century and we all shared the excitement that we were living in important times.

This importance was enhanced in my second or third year there when a relatively well-known film director advertised for extras for scenes he was recording in a ground-breaking film about the aftermath of a nuclear disaster. It was to be made on those marshes made famous in the classic David Lean film of Dickens's 'Great Expectations', a few miles from the Medway towns. Several sixth formers and younger teachers, along with many others, applied and were 'signed on'. We turned up one weekend in our tattiest clothes as requested, and all we had to do, we were told, was to make ourselves 'filthy' and then, on the command, we were to run screaming and shouting across a rough terrain. We dutifully did so – several times – and I returned home that Saturday, satisfied with my contribution, and speculating inwardly about the possibilities of a Hollywood career, as I was confident that I had been utterly convincing as a victim of a nuclear bombing. When the time came for a screening of the film, I watched avidly, waiting for that moment when I could excitedly cry: 'There I am!'.

Anti-climax followed – no sight of me on the screen could be seen! My incredibly realistic screaming and writhing apparently were to be lost to posterity for ever. I have watched that film four times and can be absolutely certain that my bit was cut! The whole film was even shown on British television recently, in 2020 I believe it was, and I could not resist seeing it again, but alas, still no sign of me! My prepared acceptance speech to BAFTA for my award has never been capable of being adapted to any other circumstances I have found myself in, I'm afraid.

It was not because the option of a career in films had been ruled out, but because, after four years of definite development, I knew I had learned so much that I felt I was ready to try to run my own English Department. I had gained a great deal from that school and from Brian, who generously supported me in my new quest. After a couple of unsuccessful interviews, I was offered the post of Head of English at a Technical High School in a town about 20 miles from the Medway towns.

When it came to my last day there, the staff gathering in the staffroom was a cheerful seasonal one, and mine was the only farewell because it was December and I was starting my new post in the Spring term

CHAPTER THREE

beginning in January. The head of the school, whom I had felt I knew little of and I assumed knew little of me, gave a speech about me, which both surprised and honoured me. 'As you know,' he said, 'David Middlewood is someone who is straight, speaks honestly and fairly, cares about his students deeply and is a trusted and professional colleague. Above all, he will always tell you the truth as he sees it and I, for one, respect him for that.'

Those were his words and I realised, yet again, how insightful some people are without their ever making you aware of how they are gaining those insights into the person you are trying to be. I was humbled by what he said, pondered and absorbed his words, and vowed that I would try to live up to them, as I took my next step on the journey up the potentially slippery slope of career advancement.

Chapter Four

SOMETHING A LITTLE MORE SENIOR

Getting One's Feet Under The Table

I took up my new post as Head of the English Department at that Technical High School in a January, where a new Headteacher had begun only two terms before. That head, I discovered, had made a career move which has become virtually impossible since, by being appointed from his previous post as Head of a Maths department, missing out the deputy headteacher stage altogether. That area of England, Kent, was one where the tripartite system envisaged by the 1944 Education Act, of Grammar, Technical and Secondary Modern schools, had actually been fully implemented. Only a very small number of areas of England provided more than the Grammar and Secondary Modern. I had been warned both when I applied for the post, and at my informal chats on

CHAPTER FOUR

my interview day at the school, that these Technical School students were not very good at English and I would find it difficult. To me that was a challenge as I refused to accept that anybody was not interested in English, or could not be made to be interested! Whatever the level of ability, and even if their interests were mainly elsewhere, I believed – and still do – that one's native language can hold a fascination for any person. I had set my feet on the path of persuading pupils to learn and love the language and literature, just as I did, wherever they went to learn. Those warnings proved needless and I spent nine happy and successful years there, trying to do that, while the schooling system underwent various reorganisations, which involved the school changing its name more than once.

Such changes of school names can be extremely helpful to aspiring teachers when they complete an application form for dispatch to a new place about a new post. It looks much more impressive on your CV and/or form if you wish to give an impression of a range of experience that the new job's details may have asked for. To illustrate with an entirely imaginary example:

'2008-2012 Wesford High School, Bardchester
2012-2016 Alderman Smith Upper School, Bardchester
2017-2020 Bardchester Oakwood Academy, Bardchester.'

Although this applicant may have remained in the same city (and why not?), he/she has taught in three different schools which shows initiative and willingness to sample new experiences!

In fact, Wesford High School will have changed its name more than once in local reorganisations, and there will be many a teacher reading this who has completed a CV in this way! No one is telling any untruths, after all! I used a little of this very technique myself in applying successfully for the Vice-principalship I describe later.

One of the first pieces of advice that was given – and still is – to many teachers, is that, when taking on any new post or even new class, you should start firmly and then you are able to relax later, because if you start in a too friendly manner, it is almost impossible to gain back the control you need for effective teaching. As a new Head of Department, it was even more important to show everyone, pupils and staff, that this new chap meant business! On my first day of teaching, the morning lessons passed satisfactorily, and after lunch break, it was time for my first class with some 16 year olds. After introductions, I told them that I had to leave the class while I fetched books from the English store cupboard, a floor below the classroom. Giving them clear instructions to be 'very quiet' in my absence, I left the room with a couple of students to help me. On my return, I could hear the noise from the top of the stairs! As I entered the room, the hubbub died down somewhat but there were many grinning faces – I was being tested!

Long before corporal punishment was officially abolished in schools in England, I had never believed in or practised any form of physical chastisement, and the advice I was to give later as a leader to staff that had relied on the cane or something similar previously was to look fierce if necessary, sound fierce, and, if you must hit something, hit the desk! One unfortunate youth in the front row was grinning more than most, as I told them,

'I thought I told you to be quiet while I was out of the room!'

and brought my hand down on this young man's desk lid with tremendous force and with a voice of apparent anger. The youth and the whole class nearly jumped from their seats, were immediately silent, and the lesson proceeded really well, with attentive and responsive learners,

CHAPTER FOUR

so good that I was able to smile and compliment and encourage. The word, of course, went round the school about the new chap:

'A good bloke but you don't want to get on the wrong side of him!' seemed to be the gist of the talk, which was fine by me.

What I have not mentioned is the agonising pain that shot through my hand and up my arm the moment my hand hit the desk! It felt as if they were on fire. I managed to half stifle the yell of pain that tried to come out of my mouth, and it probably sounded like suppressed fury to the class, fortunately. With a throbbing hand and arm, I got through the lesson well enough and even managed a joke or two to show the students that I was not all anger! I of course said not a word to any colleague about what had happened, but did not delay much after hours on my first day.

This was of course because, after school, the emergency department of the local hospital was the most obvious first port of call. An X-ray confirmed that I had sustained, or rather had self-inflicted, a hairline fracture of a bone in my hand. Nothing could be done. I was told it would 'mend itself in time', and a course of painkillers ensued. I still shared the indignity of this self-harm with no one at the school, and my reputation as a decent chap, a good teacher, and one who can be fierce if needed, suited me just fine! Oh, and one with a sense of humour, of course!

A colleague and good friend of mine, Bob, once employed a device also related to threats rather than reality to establish his reputation for firm discipline, and it was less painful than mine. In the Technical High school, most of the classrooms had a small storeroom attached inside the room, large enough for two chairs and a small table as well as books and papers. As he told the story, Bob was good friends with a man who was the father of a boy in one of his classes. The boy was somewhat troublesome, and Bob learned that the family were going on the holiday of a lifetime, provided that the son got into not one bit of trouble. If he did, the holiday was off! At the beginning of a lesson, when the previous one had threatened to become a little unruly partly due to this particular pupil, Bob harshly spoke to the boy to come into the storeroom, and he then closed the door, leaving the class agog.

'Listen,' said Bob. 'I am going to hit this table with this ruler, and each time I do, you are going to yell out as if something hurts you! If you don't do this, I am reporting your behaviour to your dad the next time I see him. No holiday for you then! Get that?'

The class heard a whack and a yell. Another and another yell! A third! The boy came out, looking thoroughly chastened, and the class was quiet and attentive when Bob followed.

When the class asked the boy about what had happened, he replied, as boys often do: 'Nothing!'

All ended well, and the holiday was taken, he understood. I should add that Bob, like myself, did not actually ever use physical punishment and he was an excellent teacher, going on to be a deputy headteacher. The boy, it seems, rather admired Bob's cunning strategy and saw himself as being part of that plan, and he went on to do well at school. I would rather like to know if he became a teacher himself, but I confess that I am unaware of this being so.

CHAPTER FOUR

Learning About Leading

Time moved on and I learned a great deal during my time as a head of department about people management in particular – which is by far the most important element of any kind of leadership, as far as I am concerned. I also made some good friends there, one of whom, Richard, I was later to link up with during my university career.

The staffroom was generally a convivial place, and its role in school culture can be underestimated. Schools and their leaders seemed to have different unwritten rules about their use. In that school, the head was NEVER to be found entering the staffroom and if, on the rarest of occasions, his upper body appeared at the door, an uncomfortable hush would descend. In other schools, principals took their coffee in the same place as staff and no one batted an eyelid.

Another interruption in those pre-mobile phone days was of course when the school office put an outside call through, asking for a particular teacher. It happened that we had a lad whose surname was Thatcher at the school and he was in one of my Sixth Form groups doing Advanced Level English. Just at that time, the Conservative government appointed a certain woman as Education Secretary, who immediately became nicknamed 'the Milk Snatcher' because it was she who abolished the milk ration to all school children, which had been in place ever since the Second World War as a nourishment for children and supplied through schools. One day, during the lunch hour, the staffroom phone rang and a nearby teacher picked it up. He listened to the secretary's request, asked for some hush and called out,

'A call for David Middlewood! Mrs Thatcher is on the phone and wants to ask you something!'

Mayhem ensued. Suggestions forthcoming included that greatness had been thrust upon me, my time had come, friends should not be forgotten when any jobs were available in the Education Ministry, and others slightly less complimentary about going from left to right! It was difficult to hear poor Mrs Thatcher when I did talk with her, dealing with some relatively minor matter about her son's progress, but the call left me with several days of simulated surprise from colleagues that I was still remaining at the school considering that call.

The most enjoyable part of my years there still lay in the teaching of English, particularly to older students. As the Head of the subject, I was able to select the books on the exam syllabus for our particular study, and I was able to indulge myself in delving into the pleasures of poets, playwrights, and novelists that my university course in English had not had room for. So, Austen, Hopkins, Tennyson, the Brontes, Hardy, Eliot, and very many others, along with Fielding, Dickens, the other Eliot, Shaw, Woolf, Wells, all led me into huge pleasures which I could relish. The joy was that having studied and taught one specific text for the exam, I could buy at home others for my own pleasure and begin to build up what is now my very substantial personal collection.

In relation to this choosing of books, I had of course noted over the years how tastes, and what was permissible, had begun to change radically since my own school days. In Chaucer at Advanced Level, for example, my own text for study at school had been the 'Prologue to The Canterbury Tales' and 'The Nun's Priest's Tale'. In the early seventies, however, one year, I was surprised – and delighted – to see that the tale for study, alongside the Prologue was 'The Miller's Tale'! Now, even among those whose knowledge of Chaucer is limited, the Miller's Tale is notorious for its bawdiness and downright smut! It is the kind of story that sent adolescents sniggering as they learn of hairy bums being stuck out of windows to be kissed – and it has farting as well! I do not

CHAPTER FOUR

exaggerate. It was an obvious choice for any English teacher to grab the attention of 17 and 18 year olds, so I got ready to order the copies.

It was the practice at that school, when those of 16 years were preparing to stay on at school and had to decide what to study at Advanced Level to have a kind of 'shop window' on one day in the Summer Term, when each Head of Subject would address the whole of that year group about the merits of studying their particular subject in the following terms. I prepared my own ten-minute spiel accordingly, trying to strike the right balance between ribaldry and genuine information. I had originally intended by referring to Forster's 'Passage To India' and Hardy's 'Tess of the D'Urbervilles', two other chosen novels, to develop a theme with sex at the centre of the whole thing, but decided that I did not want to trivialise two of my favourite novels. Instead, I would put the final emphasis on the Miller's Tale. After all, how can you trivialise a story where a man puts his nether regions out of a window and farts in another man's face? And that is without even mentioning the poker!

On the day, I became slightly apprehensive about what other colleagues might think, but thought that, as all is fair in love, war and numbers in your sixth form groups, I'd go ahead. After the joys of Art, Biology and Chemistry had been dutifully presented (it was strictly alphabetical!), I stood up and immediately scrapped my opening gambit.

'You have just heard all about the delights of studying Biology. Well, next year's English course also contains a certain amount of Biology, particularly human anatomy. And particular parts of the human anatomy that we all know about and use and always have. One book we read was written about five and a half centuries ago, but it shows something about us that we still relish.' And so on and so on.

I brought them to the Chaucerian story, carefully referring to 'parts of the human anatomy' as often as needed. Using euphemisms such as 'posterior' and 'a rush of wind from that particular part of the body', and saying that Chaucer spelled the whole thing out in plain language, I certainly had their full attention. Indeed I noticed that some of my fellow subject leaders who were sometimes prone, as I confess I was, to switch off interest when other subjects were being described, were listening quite keenly. Having described that part of the syllabus, I was moving on to the rest when I noticed that the Headteacher had appeared at the back of the hall where this event was taking place. When I had finished, he signalled to me that he wanted a word and I went over. He ushered me out of hearing and out of the hall, and said,

'Very interesting. But do you think it is completely fair to your colleagues? After all, the delights of sine and cosine couldn't possibly compete with that, could they? I hope you can cope with the numbers you get!'

He was right about the numbers anyway. Our department had its biggest ever take-up for the following term, and I am pleased to say that the final results were excellent. A few comments were made on some of the more unusual subject combinations made by some students, such as Chemistry, Physics and English, but I naturally put this down to the students' commendable willingness to widen their horizons. This is nowadays seen as liberating and altogether something to be encouraged. Some of these new English students displayed some impatience early on in the course, clearly having expected it to begin with the Miller. I was too canny for that, of course, and in fact it was not until the Summer Term that they were told they would be doing the Miller's Tale in the final year! By then, I like to think they were fully engrossed in and enjoying the literature we were studying together. Whenever I see an advert on the television or anywhere else and am

CHAPTER FOUR

ready to decry it as compete rubbish, I suppose I should remember what someone in the advertising or marketing business told me – that if it makes people buy the product, then it's not rubbish. Who am I to judge perhaps?

A Leap Into The Unknown

After those very enjoyable and I believe very successful nine years in the school as Head of English, Senior Teacher and other promoted roles which I confess had induced me to remain (I am as subject to flattery as the next person!), I felt I had to stir myself from what by now had become a very comfortable situation. Thus, I began applying for Deputy Headships and Vice Principalships. Fate, playing its usual role, decided that the one I was successful in obtaining – again after a few failed interviews – was at what was designated an 'Upper School and Community College', quite a lot further north than others I had tried for. So it was that I took up my new promoted post there one September in the late 1970s. This coeducational comprehensive school had been formed by the amalgamation of three smaller secondary schools two years earlier and was in a brand new building which was almost completed when I arrived. As the number of students was now about a thousand, another second in command in addition to the two already there had been needed. So, a second-in command I was, although strictly fourth in the pecking order of the leadership hierarchy. I vividly recall getting my very first taste of what it was like, however, to be right at the top by an episode that took place about a fortnight into my new role.

I shall never know whether it was by complete chance, or by a carefully contrived strategy for my induction as a deputy, but it so happened that on one day, the principal was at a local leaders' conference, the senior vice-principal was on a training course and the other member of the leadership team was attending the funeral of a former staff member. I was in complete charge!

'So, this is what it is like', I found myself saying to myself as I strode through the day, answering questions with what I felt was just the right tone of authority – whilst batting any really awkward ones off for the principal to deal with on his return, of course.

This particular school was a rural comprehensive and about 75 per cent of the thousand or so students travelled to and from school by hired coach or standard bus from the various villages in the area. Thus, the departure of all these at the end of the school day at 4 o'clock was a considerable and necessarily complicated operation. On this particular day, a rainy September one, at about 3.45pm, I retired to the school office to supervise through the windows the usual departure of several hundred young people as all the coaches arrived. Then the school secretary, with what seemed suspiciously like a hidden smile, said to me, whilst pointing to the area where the first coaches were due to arrive:

'That boy there, Jeffrey Stevens, he's not supposed to be on the premises. He's banned since the Principal suspended him!'
'Right,' I said, and, pulling my raincoat around me, I strode purposefully as I thought, out the door up to young Master Stevens. As I neared him, I noticed with less than enthusiasm that he was not unaccompanied, as he was holding on a lead a rather large Alsatian dog.
'Jeffrey Stevens?'
'Yeah. Who are you?'
'I am the Vice-principal, and you are not allowed on these premises. You are banned, as you perfectly well know. So, leave now and get off this site.'

CHAPTER FOUR

He hesitated and muttered something inaudible. The conversation was not exactly proceeding but it got to the point where I thought he was about to move, just as I saw the first coach drive in, ready to turn round and draw up near us. In a few moments, hundreds of children would be pouring out to that spot! It was then that I made my fatal mistake. In what I probably thought was a grand gesture, I said again, 'Now, go!' and raised my hand, pointing towards the exit.

The next second, I was aware that the sleeve of my raincoat was firmly in the strong jaws of that large Alsatian, which had leapt at my gesture and seized my pointing arm! Picture the scene if you can. It now certainly did not appear majestic or grand and all I could feel with immense relief was that I was wearing that coat. I gingerly brought my arm down with the dog still attached, and, whilst not now masterful, I was, along with being utterly terrified, pretty angry!

'And that animal's not under control. I'm getting the police and reporting it!'

Whether it was the word 'Police' or a genuine concern for his canine companion, the youth mumbled something to the dog, something else to me, which I am sure could not be written here even if I had heard it. Then, reluctantly, Master Stevens trudged away and off the site, just as the end of school bell sounded and further coaches came into view.

With as much dignity as I could muster and conscious of the very sound advice once given that, whenever you are in a dangerous situation, always remember to bring dry trousers, I made my way back to the office. The secretary, instead of offering me those congratulations which I personally felt I had well merited, said,

'You HAVE gone a funny colour, Mr Middlewood!'

My report of this incident the next day to my fellow leaders was delivered with all due modesty, as if we were all acknowledging such things were just part of a normal day's work. I was inwardly slightly put out that the principal seemed to find the whole episode rather amusing, but I thought it best to pretend I shared a small amount of his merriment. However, if I am ever tempted to get a bit above myself in terms of the authority of any position I hold, an image comes into my mind of my standing in the rain, with an Alsatian hanging off the sleeve of a coat I am wearing! In terms of heroism, I am a mere mortal with just an average share of this quality, I assure you.

Among other duties and tasks which had not been expected of me in any of my previous roles in schools was the one of being expected to lead certain assemblies. As in most large schools, these gatherings at the start of the day were done on a year by year basis, meaning that all the students of the same age were brought together, about three hundred in that particular school, to be addressed by a senior member of staff. It happened that the first one I was scheduled for was the Sixth Form. This comprised the oldest students, seventeen and eighteen year olds, and was smaller in number, about ninety to a hundred. Naturally, I wanted my first one to go well and I spent a while preparing it. I cannot now remember my chosen theme, but it was a rousing success because of a certain young lady; well, actually an imaginary one!

I had already learned in giving any kind of public address that it was important to gain – and preferably seize – your audience's attention right at the start, if you wanted to keep them listening. It was a precept that stood me in very good stead in my later career in universities, when I was required to give lectures regularly and even address teachers' conferences. If I had ever doubted it, what happened at this assembly would have converted me to the idea for ever. I had finally decided on my attention-seizing opening line, but I had certainly underestimated

CHAPTER FOUR

its impact. After being introduced to the student audience as the new vice-principal, I rose to my feet. Deliberately pausing at first, I began,

'I must begin by confessing to you that I woke up this morning with misgivings–'

I paused to allow the implication of 'Miss Givings' to sink in, and as I prepared to move on, the whole place collapsed in total howls of laughter. Even the staff members present were helpless with giggling. I did what one must do in those circumstances, not laugh at one's own humour, but raise a quizzical eyebrow and suggest perhaps a wry grin, as if you cannot really see what there is to get worked up about. I tried to continue but it was a long time before the students could be ready to attend. If they expected more jokes, they were probably disappointed, but, as I said, I do not really remember anything else about that assembly.

One unfortunate student had been designated to give me a vote of thanks afterwards, but sensibly she clearly threw away her intended script and said,

'Mr Middlewood, thank you for that. On behalf of us all, I would like to welcome you to the school and we all hope that you enjoy your time here – and the young lady as well, of course!'

The senior member of staff thanked me privately afterwards and said, 'They'll remember that one!' He was right. My reputation was made – for better or worse. I was forever known among the students as the deputy head with the miss! No member of the leadership team ever mentioned that assembly to me, and I certainly wasn't going to ask their opinion.

By chance, at a conference a few years later, I happened to see on the list of attendees a name – 'Miss E. C. Givens'. It had never occurred to me until that moment that if such a person had been on the staff roll at my college at the time when I made my pun upon that name, the students' hysteria would have been even greater at the time of the assembly, but that afterwards I would have been in the direst trouble, and my nickname, I am sure, would have been quite different! I mention this partly because, if anyone reading this is tempted to use such a joke, it would be wise to check the surnames of anyone present or relevant!

If that was my nickname with the students, I made sure that my one with staff was self-designated. As the junior member of the management hierarchy, my responsibilities inevitably included some of the more mundane ones that other deputies had been only too glad to pass on. These included 'Resources management, premises and transport arrangements', as I recall, things that today would certainly be the responsibility of a non-teaching administrator. In introducing myself at the pre-term staff meeting as the new boy, I had said that I was sure that I'd be known in the staffroom as the 'bogs and buses' Deputy. This went down well with the staff, partly because it saved them the bother of inventing a label of their own. I knew this had been a good move when I learned the nickname of the senior deputy, something along the lines of being a stuffed shirt, but more precisely relating to what kept his back so straight and a certain part of the human anatomy!

I settled in well there in my new role, especially as I was able to continue some teaching of my beloved English Literature, including at Advanced Level, where of course my students were likely to begin a lesson by politely inquiring how 'she' was these days, referring to a certain 'Miss', of course.

CHAPTER FOUR

Another new experience was that of leadership team meetings which were held on a weekly basis. On the whole, I enjoyed and learned much from these occasions. The only discomfort came in an area where I had to practise a little deception. My boss, the principal, who became a great friend of mine after his retirement, was a highly educated and intelligent man who was a gifted linguist and had studied Latin at school. He knew, of course, from my application form that I had achieved Latin at A Level at school. (He did not know that I had acquired Latin by a mark of forty one per cent when the pass mark was forty!) Confident that he now had a classical ally in the team, Ken was prone during those meetings to suddenly use a Latin phrase and – without fail on such occasions – he would say,

'That's right, isn't it, David?' or similar words.

Although I would on a very rare occasion recognise such a phrase as 'Nota Bene' or 'Pro Patria' (and that was only due to teaching Wilfred Owen's poems!), I spent four years learning how to smile knowingly and my ignorance remained hidden. I am tempted to say that Ken did this 'Ad Nauseam' but that would be just showing off! I told this story at Ken's funeral service many years later when his family honoured me by asking me to give the eulogy, and they were delighted with it, recognising so much of him in that particular tale.

I had had very little experience in my previous roles in dealing with what are called external relations, apart from the parents of students I taught, but now I learned about communicating with governors, local community representatives, and neighbours of the school. The school secretary, perhaps more impressed by my handling of the Jeffrey Stevens episode than I had realised, seemed to call on me very readily whenever a slightly sensitive public relations issue was involved – or so it seemed to me anyway. I recall that one day in my third year there she took a call while I stood in the school office, put her hand over the receiver and said to me,

'It's that woman – you know the one with the house where those boys go! She wants to complain!'

Among the various escapades that students got themselves into, no doubt all part of a plan to give me valuable management experience, we had recently had occasion to receive a report from the local police that three of our 16 year old boys , not known for their academic prowess but certainly physically well built, had been found during school hours at the house of a certain woman – how does one put this – who had previously been suspected of running what used to be described as 'a house of ill-repute'. The police had warned the boys but had suggested that the woman 'needed watching'. It was apparently 'that woman' who was calling the school.

I went next door to my own office and picked up the phone.

'Hello. I am the vice-principal here. How can I help you?'
'I've got a complaint!'

Why does one get these temptations in your head, even at the most difficult of times, to make a frivolous remark? Do not tell me I am alone. One has one's duty to do and decorum – and justice – to observe, so, ignoring the inner voice prompting me to ask her about her particular ailment, I replied,

'I'm sorry to hear that, madam. What seems to be the problem?'
''Ere, I know they're saying at your place that I am an old prostitute – and I'm not 'aving it!'

CHAPTER FOUR

For someone relatively inexperienced in public relations management, this was not easy. I thought I would begin tactfully with the easier part, giving myself time to think how I could address the trickier part of the description.

'Well, that is quite unfair, madam,' I said. 'I can tell just by your voice that you are not old at all.'

While I hesitated for a moment before moving to the much more difficult part, the woman said,

'Oh, well, that's alright then.'

And the phone went dead!

Apart from the cowardly relief I felt at having avoided the hard part, I have often speculated on the caller's logic and wondered whether it was actually the adjective 'old' that she had found offensive. I was certainly not going to pursue the matter, and she made no more calls. I was glad of this because the embarrassing thought struck me later that if she had been happy with my reply, she might ring back to the school on some matter and ask to speak that 'nice vice-principal, the one who thinks I am a young prostitute!' She never did call again, however, and my career survived!

Being the bogs and buses deputy meant I needed to build a good relationship with the school's caretaker, which I did. This was easy because he was a wonderful man and I was honoured at my leaving to be invited into his on-site house to have tea and cakes with him and his wife, the first teacher, so they said, to have ever set foot there! The mundane nature of what the role then involved gave scope for all kinds of childish humour, the stuff that is part of the staff's survival strategy in the staffroom. For example, when a delegation from the female members of staff complained about the coarse nature of the lavatory paper in their toilets, I was able to post a notice on the staffroom board, worded in the appropriate official jargon, in which I promised that I 'would get to the bottom' of this matter, and so on. In my farewell speech to the staff when I left the school, I turned the whole thing into a talk about how they all knew that what I had really wanted to be was a school caretaker! The evidence, I said, lay in all that they had seen of my moving furniture, sorting the toilets (and paper), and so on. One day, I went on, Ken, the principal, had called me in and told me that I had to face it but I wasn't going to make it as a school caretaker, despite my really good efforts, and I would have to settle for the next best thing, being a school principal! The speech was well received, especially by the principal and the caretaker, and, although it didn't happen to me in my later career, I believe there had been times as a very young teacher when I was doubtful which of those two roles did actually wield the greater authority!

During my fourth year as a second in command, I had by that time acquired sufficient confidence in myself to try to obtain a post as the head or principal of a school of my own. It was time to apply! After a few attempts (you will know by now I mean failures!), I was summoned for interview for the principalship of a very large school in a town relatively near to my current school and my home. This town had, and still has, a reputation for being a 'tough' one and still features regularly in reports and records of Britain's more challenging urban areas, with high crime rates and levels of social and economic deprivation. I noted in the job details sent to applicants that the school was currently being led by an acting principal, Mrs Quinn. This usually alerts external candidates to the possibility that this might be one of those 'insider' jobs where the involvement of external candidates might be for window dressing purposes only.

CHAPTER FOUR

However, I, along with five others, arrived for interview, and any apprehensions about an inside job were somewhat allayed by learning that two of the five had been flown in from overseas forces schools where they were already principals. Surely, the authority would not spend such sums on travel expenses merely for face-saving purposes! On the second day's afternoon, the formal final interviews commenced with an august gathering of seven worthies on the appointments panel. My own interview seemed to go pretty well and we all awaited the outcome.

Time passed; we were told that the panel was still debating and there had been a delay. This delay in making the decision went on-and on! It was a good two hours, with everyone thoroughly restless, before an embarrassed education officer emerged to announce that with regret that the panel had been unable to agree and therefore no appointment would be made today! 'If we wished to re-apply etc, etc.'

We were all very annoyed; it is one thing for someone else to be preferred to yourself, but when you are all apparently judged inadequate, feelings run high. I recall that the overseas candidates in particular were understandably furious. Several years later, I discovered through an informal chat with the Authority officer that Mrs Quinn and I had received three votes each from the panel, and the seventh member had been objected to 'on a point of order' because he had left the proceedings without hearing the sixth candidate! The officer maintained that the member concerned had said he was going to vote for me, which meant the job would have been mine, so he maintained, but the process had to be declared invalid.

About a fortnight after that particular debacle, I was telephoned at home by an Authority officer saying that the post of principal there was about to be re-advertised and it was strongly hoped I would apply for it again. I had to tell the truth, which was that in the meantime I had accepted the headship of another school in another area and therefore was unavailable. This headship, of course, is the subject of the next chapter, but the main reason for recounting my near miss at this job is what I happened to read in a national newspaper about a year and a half later. The headline was:

'PARENT JAILED FOR BREAKING HEAD'S JAW'

It seemed that the man who had eventually landed the principalship at that school had in his first term been violently attacked by a student's father, high on drugs, who had pushed into the office and assaulted him! Clearly, this was in no sense any kind of laughing matter, but, given how close it seemed I had come to obtaining that post, I was able to reflect on the very thin line between what is and what could have been, and perhaps it was only the fates that were laughing at us all. I have sometimes wondered just what Mrs Quinn thought about it all. As it was, I had my new job to begin, and this time right at the top!

Chapter Five

IT'S TOUGH AT THE TOP

Getting there

Standing in the corridor outside my new office on the very first day of my tenure as the new head of the school, I was acutely aware that this was my 'honeymoon' period when the school briefly appeared to be running itself without any help from me. I was right about the brevity, by the way, because the next day brought a blazing row with the long-serving deputy head! But just for a moment there was a chance to reflect on the process that had brought me there and one that brings most school leaders to their fate, the pathway of recruitment, selection and appointment.

In England, the system, if it can be called a system, is a free-for-all, whereby candidates can apply for as many leadership jobs as they like and take their chance, according to the preferences of the Board of Governors, sponsors, Local Authorities, depending on the type of school. This is what is known as the free market approach, of course. In some countries, school principals are appointed centrally, then allocated to a specific school, often for a fixed period. In others, experienced teachers simply apply in writing to the education ministry and are appointed on the basis of that application alone, without even the interview which is a staple feature of most of the appointment processes elsewhere.

While arguments can be put forward for any of these systems as to which is the most effective in choosing the ultimate gold medal winner, the big advantage of the English system is that everyone who applies is guaranteed at least a silver medal! It might surprise you to read this, but if you have ever been in a school staffroom the day after a teacher at whatever level has been for a job interview at another school and is naturally asked by colleagues how they got on, the answer is invariably:

'I didn't get it – but I didn't like the whole thing and didn't want it anyway.'

OR

'I didn't get it, but I did very well and was told I came second.'

The former can be taken with a pinch of salt, because if you didn't like it, you were entitled to withdraw before the final part of the process.

The second explanation is a safe one, and no one can check it out, because the whole process is confidential and only the person selected

CHAPTER FIVE

is announced to the world at large. Thus, I have long suspected that staffrooms are full of people who came runners-up in their quests for headship or indeed any other promoted post. If there are six candidates at a selection interview, my estimate is that four or five of them came second! I have tried to avoid that expression myself after interviews when I failed to be offered the post. The very best interview I ever gave for a headship post in the East of England left me on a high as I left the room after a panel's questioning. Another candidate, however, was called in to be offered the post and I felt dejected. When the senior education officer, a national figure at that time, gave me feedback he told me I had given a 'brilliant' interview – yes, actually 'brilliant'! BUT, he went on to say, 'Mr Weston walked on water and they had to give it to him. I would very much welcome another application from you for another headship in this region.'

I remember that alliteration of 'Weston walked on water' so well, and I am sure I could have claimed to have come second, but fortunately no one but my wife knew I had applied there so she alone was able to admire my imaginary silver medal!

My contention of so many people coming second was confirmed after I had been successful in being selected at Deputy Head level in a community college, where there had been two internal candidates in the final six who were interviewed. When I took up the post, and later got to know both of these people as colleagues, I discovered that they had both been told they came second to me!

Whilst nearly everyone would include a sense of humour as being on the essential list of qualities needed for success as a school leader, I have only once encountered it as an actual topic during an interview. On the first day of a two-day process of appointing a new principal, when a series of mini-interviews took place with various governors, I was asked by a female governor what was clearly her 'special' question:

'Now, tell me, Mr Middlewood, how would you describe your own sense of humour?'

Perhaps I should have been prepared for this one, but I confess I wasn't. However, with what I thought was quick-thinking, I gave my reply in a single word.

'Succinct!'

Now, feeling rather pleased with myself at this witty and pithy answer, I awaited her response.

An awkward silence ensued, and it slowly dawned on me that she was expecting me to expand on this brief and, as she clearly felt, inadequate answer. I, on the other hand, felt that if I added anything it would defeat the whole point of my response and the impact of my incomparable wit would be lost. Of course, it had already been lost on that lady – and with it no doubt any chance I had of landing that particular job.

On another occasion, when I attended a two-day selection process with five other candidates, an education officer told us – or perhaps 'warned' would be a better way of putting it – that the Chair of the Board of Governors insisted at lunch on the first day that all the candidates should move tables after each of the three courses so that all governors could have the chance to talk informally with all candidates. Feeling already, as one does on these occasions, that we were being assessed on our management of peas on the cutlery, and recalling an awkward incident on such an occasion when a so-called 'concrete pudding' flew off a plate to the floor because there was no custard to hold it there, I approached the whole thing apprehensively,

CHAPTER FIVE

as I know others did. I and one other candidate sat at one table, and so on, for the first course. After the soup starter, we two rose to move to another table. Unfortunately, we went to different tables which I am sure of course was my rival's error. Another candidate gallantly offered to join me, perhaps glad to change partners for all I knew, and the second course was thus arranged. However, inevitably when we moved for the dessert course four of us arrived at the same table! Chaos followed, with some governors complaining they had not met this one or that, and others claiming they had already seen so and so. The rather flustered Chairperson declared that such a problem had never occurred previously and seemed to imply we were all clearly not very bright and probably not fit to lead a bus queue, let alone a school. I cannot remember who actually did get the job – except that it was not me – and the five rejections slipped away at the end of the day, muttering to each other, of course, that we wouldn't have wanted the rotten job anyway!

My own wife, Jacqui, had an embarrassing episode during her interview for the headship of a particular primary school. Jacqui was and still is a beautiful woman, petite and slim, but no one could deny that she was at that time anything but VERY short-sighted. Vanity prevented her wearing glasses and we have had various odd things occurring during our time together caused by her short sightedness, including getting into the wrong parked car outside a supermarket and briefly raising the hopes of the elderly male driver that he might gain from some form of a game of wife-swapping, and on another occasion mistaking the gender of a particular teacher colleague at a school assembly. On this interview occasion, she came to the end of a typical panel interview, and rose from her chair to leave the school staff room where the interview was taking place. She felt the interview had on the whole gone very well, but naturally it had been a stressful time and her hands, not to put too fine a point on it, were sweaty. As she says, never mind the 'perspiring' or 'glowing', as in the old adage, 'I was sweaty!'

As she seized the brass doorknob to leave the room, she found to her horror that she could not open the door because her hands kept sliding round the doorknob. Eventually, trying to make the best of it, she turned to the panel members and said, in as joking a tone as she could manage,

'Well, you will have to give me the job now, as I can't get out of the room!'

After a few titters from some of the members, a calm reply came from one governor:

'I am afraid you would not get out even if you opened that door. You are trying to get into the store cupboard!'

The speaker then rose, went to the real exit door, opened it, and waited for her to leave. She had to make the best she could of a less than dignified retreat.

The final thing I am forced to note is that Jacqui was offered and did get that job anyway, although I am not sure what point that story proves. My wife did have the rather annoying habit of getting each job she went to be interviewed for, unlike we lesser mortals who have to fall back on a claim that we learn by our failures. When I point this out to her, she hastily tells me how she failed often to get the part she craved in auditioning for a play to perform in, so she does know something about not being chosen. I sometimes wonder if it was because her short-sightedness caused her to say her audition piece to the listener's rear, but I say nothing!

Jacqui's attempted witticism about not getting out of the room brings me back to the interview circumstances under which I obtained the

CHAPTER FIVE

headship of the school where I enjoyed a one-day honeymoon. I and six other candidates arrived for the two-day selection process at the comprehensive school, and spent the first day in the usual routine of going round the place, learning its history and having mini-interviews with various small groups. On the afternoon of the second day, it was time for the interviews with the august panel of Governors, Councillors, and Education Authority officers, about seven or eight in total. We went in for interview in alphabetical order and, being an M, I was unsurprisingly right in the middle, fourth of seven. I remember that the person before me was in the interview room longer than the 30 minutes we had been told each of us would have, and I recall that those of us waiting or already seen were speculating that he had probably got the job in the bag! I was called in at 2: 47 pm precisely.

After introductions by the chairperson, the first question was a standard one and therefore one to be expected and prepared for.

'Well now, you have been here yesterday and this morning and looked around the school. What do you think makes you believe you could be the right leader for this school?'

I began my more or less prepared answer, knowing that far trickier ones lay ahead.

'Well, as I looked around and, thinking about my previous experience, quite a few bells rang for me–'

I got no further because, at that precise moment, the bells rang! It was a lesson change time and the bells sounded loudly and about six times.

Everyone in the room burst out laughing and continued chortling until the bells ended. Seizing the moment, I rose to my feet, spread out my arms, and said, 'Do you need any more than this?'

This also seemed to go down well and it was quite a while before things could settle to any kind of normality. From then on, it seemed I could do little wrong, although I do not recall many other questions. Perhaps this had been my turn to walk on water! I was offered the post at the end of it all and accepted. Afterwards, I reflected that if the candidate before me had not overrun his time (and the officer told me later he had talked himself out of the job by being too verbose!), I would not have gone in at that precise time to have the bells' divine intervention.

Such are some of the hazards of the open market system of selection of school leaders, where fate and coincidence may play such crucial roles.

FEET UNDER THE DESK

I spent nine years as headteacher of that school before eventually taking up what in effect turned out to be a new career as described in the next section of this book. Some of the comic episodes that occurred during those years were caused by my personal sense of humour, my own naivety, or of course by the antics of staff, students or parents.

Coming firmly into the first category was the occasion when I performed my famous – or perhaps infamous – 'striptease' at a regional headteachers' conference. The school leaders' association at that time to which I belonged held an annual conference, where about a hundred or so school leaders assembled and debated current issues. At the end of the agenda which was sent out for attendees was an item, always briefly reported on, about the charity benevolent fund for school teachers, when a collection would be taken as delegates left the room. For a reason I will explain shortly, I quietly asked the Chairperson before

CHAPTER FIVE

we began whether he would allow me to speak to that final item for a couple of minutes. He was surprised but gratefully agreed as he was spared the task of asking for money. As the conference grew to its close after a full day, the chair announced,

'And finally, and briefly, ladies and gentlemen, the Benevolent Fund and Mr David Middlewood.'

As is normal at the end of any conference, some delegates were already mentally in an armchair at home, back at school for urgent work, or for all I know at their local pub; they were certainly half out of their seats in a race to the car park. I went up on to the platform and, as I began to speak, I removed my jacket. I should say I had deliberately arrived in collar, tie and three-piece suit with waistcoat. I said that it was essential that in order to say what I had to say, I would need to remove some clothes, in fact most of my clothes!

This, as I anticipated, attracted immediate attention and the delegates half out of their seats sat down again. I said I hoped not to offend anyone, of course, but really the benevolent fund was so important and did such good work that –. I doubt whether anyone was listening to my words by this time, and I do not recall anything else I said at that point, but I continued to remove my tie, then my shoes, and to unbutton my shirt and unbuckle my trouser belt. My shirt I kept pulled across when unbuttoned and I unzipped my trousers. The reactions in this high level gathering were interesting by this time. There were some grins, one or two raucous cheers, a gasp or two, and even a peeking through fingers by one of my neighbouring colleague female headteachers. At the final moment, I threw off my shirt, and dropped my trousers to my ankles to reveal – myself in full running kit of vest and shorts, with the words 'SPONSOR ME' emblazoned across my chest!

I do not ever expect to receive a better round of spontaneous applause than the one which I got then. Indeed, I have spoken and been received well at various conferences since, but nothing could beat that one. Perhaps there was a sense of relief as well as support in the generous acclaim, but in any case delegates were vastly generous in sponsoring me in my running in the London Marathon of 1982, for that indeed was what it was all about. It was only the second year of what has become a worldwide famous annual event where many thousands take part. Then, it was a smaller key event and I with three boyhood friends had been inspired by watching the inaugural one in 1981. Our applications for entry had been accepted because the process of being accepted was more amateurish then, although there were still a few thousand who participated. I still recall the huge gale of laughter that swept through those few thousand gathered at the start when the cannon sounded to begin the marathon –and no one could move! I remember timing myself and it took six and a half minutes to get up to the starting line! As for my group of friends, we did not even find each other on the day! Marathon running for ordinary people was much rarer then, and like others in those early days, I became a minor local celebrity with my photo in the local paper and being invited to talk to local groups. I did complete the course, collect my medal and raise a very respectable sum of money for that Benevolent Fund!

Nothing could surpass the impact I made at the conference when I think about that London Marathon – except for one thing – it provided me with what turned out to be the perfect and successful chat-up line with the opposite sex! A lovely young primary school headteacher in the same town where I led the secondary school had attracted my attention, and I found an excuse to visit her at her school. While we talked in her office, the marathon was of course mentioned, and I knew that she had covered half a marathon length course with friends to raise some cash for school funds.

'How would you like to join a local marathon club?' I asked.
'How many are likely to be in it?' she innocently inquired.
'Well, if you join, there'll be two of us,' I responded.

Our training began with a drink together, and to miss out many details, whatever you may think of this approach of mine, I claim that its success is in the fact that Jacqui (yes, it was she!) and I have enjoyed more than thirty six years of happy marriage at the time of writing! Fate again perhaps? Some bells, a greasy brass doorknob and a marathon run! Who can make sense of all that?

Being more inclusive

Taking over at the helm of a school that was on my arrival essentially old-fashioned with many long-serving staff obviously brought its own special challenges, but, as a relatively young leader, I was determined that my leadership style would be more democratic and inclusive. One of my first tasks had been to re-arrange the head's office to reflect a more welcoming ambience. Instead of the leader being ensconced behind a desk to face all incomers, I moved it, in line with what is now common practice, so that my desk faced the wall, enabling me to swivel to welcome visitors, with no intervening barriers. On one occasion in the first month in my new post, I almost had cause to regret the lack of such barriers.

My secretary, who could access me without using the main door to my office, suddenly announced loudly, one morning,

'Mr Patten's at the door!'

I had not had the pleasure of that particular father's company up to now, although I was aware that there were at least two boys with that surname on the school roll. To say that Mr Patten was AT the door was actually not an accurate description because he was in fact already THROUGH the door. In fact, it was surprising that the door was still on its hinges, given the force with which it had been opened. Barely had the secretary had time to utter the words:

'And Floyd is with him.' (Floyd being one of the sons, aged 16)

before a very large man strode towards me, with the secretary still hissing, 'and the father's deaf mute!'

This at least explained Floyd's presence as an interpreter but of more immediate concern was the very large fist that his father seemed to be preparing to present to me. Given that, as I later discovered, Mr Patten was a former heavyweight boxer who had five sons, each of whom was named after a former heavyweight world boxing champion, you will surmise that I am not exaggerating when I say his fist or hand was 'very large'. Pausing only for a brief regret about changing the furniture in my office and thereby removing my desk as a barrier, I took what seemed to be the only possible action, reached out my own hand and shook his vigorously. My own hands are quite large but they felt almost dainty in his own enormous mitts.

'Good morning, Mr Patten, good to see you. Nice of you to come in –' and so on, I heard myself saying with what I hoped was a firm tone. My resolve was now slightly stiffened when I spotted his son looking as I thought rather smug with the suggestion of a snigger on his face. I glared at him, but my main concern was to keep a firm hold on his father's hand. Now, I am a simple heterosexual male, and not generally given to holding men's hands for more than a quick shake, but I held

CHAPTER FIVE

that hand for an age, all the time shaking it up and down and asking what seemed to be the problem. It gradually emerged via Floyd and signals between him and his father that the son had been the victim of some outrageous injustice brought about by one teacher, to whom it appeared his father was capable of administering severe punishment himself if the injustice were not righted by myself. I later found that Floyd was the unlucky victim of such injustices on a regular basis and readers who have worked in schools will be able to classify him at once as a particular type of scholar! We eventually seemed to have reached some form of agreement whereby I would 'look into the matter' and the father departed. Floyd was, fortunately for me, in his final year at school and only Louis (named after Joe Louis, of course!) remained, aged 12. Louis was a pleasant kind of lad, giving little cause for concern, and although I certainly gave no favours in his direction, I confess to always taking an enlightened interest in his progress-in an avuncular sort of way, you understand. As for Mr Patten, I only ever saw him once more in my time at the school. It was at a parents' evening for the year that his final son at the school was in, and, walking around a hall speaking casually to any waiting parents, I saw him sitting next to Louis and watching a teacher's lips intently. I passed within his sight and he briefly looked up, saw me and gave me a large grin. Somehow that grin meant something to me, as I smiled back and moved on. I had, long after his first visit to me, when the internet arrived, looked him up as a boxer. His record was of a very minor spot in sporting history, and it suggested an early retirement caused by the kind of injuries that we are only beginning to understand today. Whatever his record, I shall never forget that handshake!

The unfortunate muteness of Mr Patten was, of course, in stark contrast to many parents who feel they have something to draw to the school leader's attention. Like, for example, the large tattooed father who swept into Jacqui's office one day to complain bitterly about the bad language that his son was picking up from 'her' school. Furthermore, the dad went on to say, he knew bloody well where it was coming from; it was from, I quote:

'That bloody little sod, Billy Johnson!'

It was hard to argue with the fact that his son was certainly getting his bad language from somewhere!

Ups and Downs – Ins and Outs

An unusual feature of the office I had rearranged for democratic reasons was that it had two doors for entry and exit. The building which held my office was an ugly post-war block, and in addition to the main access door used by everyone, there was another mostly metal door, presumably some kind of fire door. Floor length curtains concealed it and I do not think I had even noticed it on my preliminary visits to the school in the Summer Term prior to actually taking up my new post. However, I soon saw the opportunities that having two exits offered – and I do not mean merely evading an unwelcome visitor! I believe I only slipped out that way on one occasion for that reason when I heard the tones of the local pompous bore ready to hold forth on the degeneracy of today's youth, compared with his own times, when of course everything had been sweetness and light. Not being in the mood for hearing yet again about how a good hiding had not done him any harm, and yet again having to resist the temptation to point out that the evidence pointed exactly the other way, I left by that door. I was just in time to hear the secretary say: 'Oh dear, he's not there. I must have missed him popping out.'

CHAPTER FIVE

However, the most useful aspect by far of having an extra exit door was when it came to interviewing suspected miscreants. I have probably watched too many police dramas on television, but I had learned that the golden rule in interrogating more than one suspect is not to let them collude, especially after the first one has been questioned. There had been an incident involving some damage in a laboratory and, based on information received, the Deputy Head and I were confident that we knew the three boys concerned. They were denying the accusation, however, and we decided to interview the three of them, individually of course. The best way I can describe this is by giving a taste of some of the dialogue between the boys (Johnson, Manson and Young) and myself and the Deputy. We interviewed Johnson first and it became clear that he was guilty but refused to admit it, obviously afraid of 'telling on' his partners in crime.

'Right, Johnson. You can go for now. I hope you will think carefully about this and come back to me when we have seen the others.'

Clearly, his only chance was to all stick to the same story.

'Off you go! Straight back to class. No, not that way, Johnson. Show him out, Mr Howard.'

The Deputy pulls the curtains back and a bewildered Johnson departs through the new door. The curtains are pulled back in place.

Manson enters, looks around and is clearly astonished not to see his pal, Johnson, in the room.

'Now, John Manson, did you cause this lab damage or not? Just you, or with the others?'

'No, sir,' is the reply while his eyes constantly search the room, as if expecting Johnson to emerge from behind a filing cabinet or jump out of a wastepaper basket.

'Pay attention, John Manson, and please look at me while I am talking to you! Can you hear me alright, or have you lost something?'

'Yes, sir. I mean, no sir. I was wondering something, sir?'

'Wondering what?'

'Where Johnson is, sir?'

'Oh, he's gone.'

'Gone, sir?'

'Yes, gone. Are you losing your hearing as well as your eyesight?'

'What do you mean, 'gone', sir?'

'It means he is not here, John Manson. Are you pretending you are stupid now? I know you are actually an intelligent young man, which is why I am surprised at your getting involved in this damage incident.'

'It was an accident, sir!'

The breakthrough comes! We hear Manson's account.

'You can go now – the same way as Johnson.'

Manson looks rather worried at that prospect as if he is to be whisked away into some outer space capsule, and is almost relieved when Mr Howard opens the new door and shows him out, pulling the curtains back across after him.

Young is then summoned and as he enters the room, he is even more astonished than his friend before him to find that NEITHER of his co-conspirators is in the room!

'Well, Stephen Young, this need not take long. We now know that it is claimed to be an accident, involving all three of you and it would have

CHAPTER FIVE

saved a lot of trouble if you had had the courage to own up at once. Are you listening to me, Stephen? Why are you looking all over the place and not at me?'

'Yes, sir. I mean it was an accident, and I am sorry, sir. Sir?'

'Yes, Stephen?'

'Only I thought Johnson and Manson were in here?'

'They were. Quite correct.'

'But they are not here now, sir.'

'Quite right, Stephen. They are not. At least your eyesight is in good order, then.'

'Yes, sir. Thank you, sir. Please, sir, can I ask where they have gone?'

'Obviously, back to their classroom – which is where you must go now. Tell the other two that you are all three to come to Mr Howard's office straight after school today, and we'll sort out what you need to do to make up for the damage.'

Young exits by the normal door, by which he entered. I was not party to the discussions the three of them had in or after class, but they all turned up as ordered after school. It was time for we two adults to indulge ourselves with a chuckle, and a feeling of satisfaction that we had done our small bit to add to the enduring belief about some teachers having almost magical powers that are beyond the understanding of mere pupils or students!

Of course, we teachers, whatever our special powers, are so often mere parents ourselves, and this can be a testing experience for both parties at times. My own sons' journeys through schooling were not without incident, since, thank goodness, they were normal students, and of course that meant with the usual mixture of good and bad! Perhaps, schools were wary of too much contact with a parent who was head of a school elsewhere, but I did become quite involved with one secondary school in particular, and after initial suspicion, the principal there and

I became convivial allies. I recall receiving a phone call from the Head of Year at that school about my son, Stephen, 14 years old at the time. Apparently, he had found a way of manipulating a vending machine in the school, so that it received certain dud coins and was quietly doing a solid business in selling – at a reduced price – these coins to his classmates. The Head of Year was a man I had a good deal of respect for, and we had an amicable conversation about the matter where I, of course, supported the school's action. Off the record, and not to be passed on to my son, we shared a discussion about the promising signs of business acumen his scheme had displayed, and how we thought he showed promise in such an area. Incidentally, this was confirmed when on leaving school at sixteen, and buying an 'old banger' of a motorbike for fifty pounds, he crashed the bike within two weeks and managed to sell the pieces of it that remained for sixty pounds! Perhaps the Head of Year and I were right!

Another of my democratising procedures as leader in my new school was to try to get the staff to use first names of students rather than surnames (I did mention it was an old-fashioned school!). Having insisted the students could actually remain indoors at breaktimes (another revolutionary practice), I took to mingling with them at morning break and getting to know them more informally. Thus, it happened one day, I met one fifteen year old with a shaven head (punks were still in vogue then) and asked him his name.

'Saber, sir,' he said.
'No, I mean your first name.'
'Anus!'

Not knowing whether I had misheard or the young man was simply telling me to mind my own business in his own way, I was for once lost for words and beat a hasty retreat to the school office to consult the

CHAPTER FIVE

registers. I found 'Saber' – now first name?

'Here it is – Aeneas.' Surprise indeed! I remembered my Virgil and assumed there were various spelling forms. The lad did not strike me as a natural classical scholar, but one must not be lookist, as we are constantly reminded today.

The next time I saw Aeneas, he was in a conversation with some classmates, and I distinctly heard more than one of them address him as 'Anus'. I asked various staff, but of course they had only ever used his surname and it was obvious a few of them thought I had brought any such problem on myself by asking such questions and it therefore served me right!

I got to know young master Saber reasonably well over the next year or so, and managed to produce a pronunciation of his first name that seemed to satisfy us both, a kind of AAnEEEAS! I think he just thought I was being posh, but we got along pretty well, so much so that when he was due to leave school, he asked to see me and asked my advice on a private matter.

'Can I ask you, sir, how you go about changing your name?'

I explained that you can do this very easily, and mentioned the options, including legal processes.

Taking a fatherly interest, I asked him what he was thinking of changing it to. He replied, 'Rip.' This was the second time he had rendered me speechless!

Whether he ever did change it, I did not find out, but as I reflected, he had done remarkably well to make his way through childhood and adolescence without suffering the mockery that many others would have done in such a situation. His muscular build and fearsome glare might possibly have helped, I suppose – but who says a classical education is of no value!

Mentioning my secretary's anxiety when telling of Mr Patten's arrival reminds me of two other occasions when something caused her to be in what we knew of as 'a high old state'. The first was when we, like many other schools locally, and even nationally, were experiencing a spate of hoax alarm calls about bombs being on the premises, just as occasional bouts of fire alarm raising could break out. As instructed by the Education Authority, we were obliged to obey all such alarms or calls, and obviously the delight of seeing the whole school disrupted was the reason for the miscreant causing it all.

We had a student, a 15 year old boy, called Jason Powell, as I recall, who had been temporarily suspended from school for quite a serious offence. On this occasion, the secretary, rushing into my office, said,

'There's someone in a call box needs to speak to you. I'm pretty sure it's Jason Powell!'

I went into the school office to take this call.

'Hello, is that you, Jason?'
'Never you mind who it is! 'ere, you listen!'
'I am listening.'
'This is serious. This is one of them bomb calls; you know, the 'oax calls!'

Somehow, I didn't think Jason had yet got the hang of terrorism or proper threatening behaviour, or whatever he saw himself espousing,

CHAPTER FIVE

and I felt completely justified on this occasion in ignoring the official advice about vacating the premises. I even resisted the temptation to raise the matter with him when his suspension was over and he returned to school. I would have followed his subsequent career with interest, but somehow I had deduced that Jason was not one of the world's great communicators and dialogue between us was never all that successful.

The other occasion when my secretary was rendered positively inarticulate was when she buzzed through to me to say something about a son being on the phone – or so I thought. Now I have four sons, so I was trying to get her to tell me which one of them it was calling me before I realised she was referring to 'The SUN', the redtop, the tabloid, infamous for Page Three topless girls and much else besides in those days. I calmed her, steadied myself and took the call from a very well spoken man, who was saying something about a story that had come down from 'the regional press'.

The story was about an incident earlier that week (today being a Friday) which had involved my excellent young Head of History and his teachers having taken about a hundred students by coach to a London museum. Five boys had skived off, got tipsy on some cider, and missed the coach back! They had been forced to make their way back to the hometown by rail, and had been already seen and dealt with by myself on their return to school.

The reporter asked various questions, 'in the public interest' of course:

'Do you support the teacher?' – 'Completely. Yes.'
'Will you still be allowing such outings?' – 'Definitely. Yes.'

After some odd questioning about my age, so it could appear in brackets after my name, in that peculiar practice of some parts of the press, the reporter rang off and told me that they would almost certainly be running the story.

The next day being Saturday, I of course needed to find out whether we would be 'in The Sun'. It was necessary to buy a copy. Choosing my attire carefully and, deciding that dark glasses and a mackintosh with a turned up collar, and pulled down hat were unsuitable because they would make me look like some seedy top shelf magazine seeker, I went to the local newsagent to get my usual paper – plus a copy of The Sun. Outside, I quickly scanned the pages. At least not front page! No, not Page Three – that's a relief!

Ah, here we are – Page Seven ! Huge headline:
'BOYS GO ON A CIDER BENDER!'

The report was, I had to admit, factually accurate and my own remarks were correctly reported. Looking more closely, I saw that the whole of Page Seven was given over to various misdemeanours that had occurred in comprehensive schools around the United Kingdom, most of them some time ago – a suicide of a young girl in Cardiff who had gone to such and such a school, two girls from a particular school arrested for shoplifting in Sheffield, a boy from a school in Ipswich who had set fire to some waste ground near a house, and so on. I drew my own conclusions, remembered the public school tones of the reporter I had spoken to, reflected on my own and others' prejudices and was able to go to school on Monday ready to face anything!

The staff of any school, as well as possessing the professional attributes they have in common, are as humans, the same mixture as most groups of people are, as far as a sense of humour is concerned. There are the staff room jokers, those with an ironic view on education, those that try to see humour in almost every situation, and a small group of those with absolutely no sense of humour at all. People in this category often unfortunately become the butt of students' and colleagues' jokes themselves, very likely not being able to be aware of it.

I recall one such teacher who had a formidable knowledge of his subject matter (one of the sciences), but also a deserved reputation for lessons which, to put it as politely as possible, lacked excitement. His redeeming feature was that he knew of this deficiency in himself and would say to someone telling him a joke, 'Sorry, I don't get it!' with such honesty that he would be forgiven. So, he went on his steady, rather pedestrian way, and I remember that it fell to me once to have a 'professional discussion' with him about his teaching and his likely progress in his chosen career. We were proceeding cautiously and I posed the question as to whether it was at all possible for him to be more animated in his teaching. After all, I pointed out, he knew his stuff very well, was probably inwardly pleased about it, and did he not think it might be an asset if he wished his career to prosper to show just a little more drive or energy?

He pondered my point carefully for several seconds and then said:

'You know, there could be something in what you are saying. My wife has said to me that what I need is a bomb behind me before I get round to doing anything.'

His delivery of this marital suggestion was so lugubrious that it was hard for me not to smile at the picture it conjured. I made a jesting remark about myself and his wife getting together on this subject, but that was a mistake, because, as I should have known, he took it quite literally.

Again, after pondering what he saw as my suggestion, he said:

'Thank you, but I don't think my wife would like that; she likes to keep home and work quite separate.'

I admitted this was very wise and moved on, but I could never see him again without having that flash of insight into his domestic situation.

There was one other occasion when, having been the intended butt myself, I managed, with that same teacher's accidental help, to turn the tables. On a tip-off from one of my deputies, I learned that it was the staff room practice after I had been there about five years to take wagers on the exact time that my end of term address to the whole school in the large sports hall would finish! It was a gentle way, I realise, of their being able to maintain interest in my stirring rhetoric as the afternoon drew to a close and the beginning of the holidays beckoned. Having found out who was holding the purse for the winner when known, I approached him and suggested that it would be good fun if, during our final staff meeting of the term, when we said farewell to those teachers leaving, I made an official presentation to the winner of this particular sweepstake. It was agreed and, as we gathered afterwards, the organiser told me that the winner was Jeremy, the science teacher! I reached that point in the proceedings in the staff room and then said solemnly that there was one more presentation to make, stated what it was, and announced Jeremy as the winner! As he shuffled to the front to receive the cash, accompanied by loud applause, I could almost swear I saw a glimmer of a smile around his mouth. What an occasion! Once again, I overdid it – I made a joke!

'And, Jeremy,' I said, 'don't forget the commission you owe me on giving you the right time. We'll keep it between ourselves, of course!'

CHAPTER FIVE

Jeremy turned with a puzzled look on his face.

'Oh, how much is that then?' he said. Gales of laughter followed and I assured Jeremy the money was ALL his!

Those end of term staff gatherings were, of course, an opportunity to say farewell and thanks to those staff members leaving, either for other posts or retirement. Whilst the vast majority of these were an extremely pleasant part of a leader's duties, there were a few occasions which called for much careful preparation, and were valuable in honing one's rhetorical skills. These, of course, were the ones where the person leaving was not exactly known for energy, or enthusiasm or originality. I discovered that the best way to deal with it was to find out about some activity unrelated to education or schools at which they either excelled or were keen on, and wax lyrical about this. Thus I have held forth about pigeon fancying, cricket scoring, and, memorably, ballroom dancing, all of which are worthy activities but whose chief merit here was its sheer unrelatedness to schools. Thus, one retiring member of the caretaking staff, famous within educational circles for his ability to move dust from one place to another and regard that as a good day's work, I found out to be a very able ballroom dancer, in partnership with his wife. Thus, I was able to paint a pretty and flattering picture of the two of them in the future, post-retirement, circling the floor, he holding his wife instead of a broom, in a way which would bring back memories of his caretaking, but in a much more profitable way. Everyone seemed very happy at my efforts, although for different reasons among the audience, of course.

Often, animals are a source of humour and it so happens that both the Technical High School when I arrived there as Head of English and the school where I became the head had a small 'farm' on site. The 'Agricultural Studies' on the curriculum of the former soon disappeared as the school put more emphasis on academic success, and opportunities in careers in that field diminished. The 'farm' in the latter school took the form of a kind of outhouse with a range of creatures resident, such as rabbits, chicken, ducks and a goat. The teacher in charge was very committed to them and I admit the students who took an interest were equally so. Two images stick in my mind, however. The fact that the poultry tended there seemed to decrease in population over the festive Christmas season always, wrongly I am sure, made me conjure a picture of some members of staff tucking into part of the curriculum with more relish on Christmas Day than on any other occasion. The second image, less easily dislodged from my mind, is of when the school goat collapsed and the inconsolable teacher told me of its demise, despite his having attempted to resuscitate it via the 'kiss of life'! Bearing in mind a goat's typical diet, which consists of just about anything within reach, this is not a tasteful image, although some might see it as heroic. Certainly, when I told the story to my primary headteacher wife, Jacqui, she reminded me that her close encounter with her school's pet goat had been when it had eaten half her skirt away just prior to her taking a full school assembly. Needless to say, the pupils found it hilarious!

A fitting way perhaps to end this particular chapter will be to report a humorous remark made by someone far more august than myself or anyone else mentioned to date, one of Her Majesty's Inspectors (HMI). These were the days before OFSTED existed in England as the schools' inspection regime, and until the 1990s, the only form of inspection of schools that occurred, apart from some Local Authority visits, were ones carried out by HMI. These inspections were relatively rare, and many teachers and Headteachers would go through their whole career without undergoing one. Indeed, it was a joke in some staffrooms until the 1990s that if you moved at the right times you could miss HMIs altogether!

CHAPTER FIVE

However, it was my fate that after just two years into my headship, I was informed by the Local Education Authority that our school had been selected for an HMI inspection. These visits lasted about four days when a team of HMIs descended and visited every area of the school, curriculum, standard of teaching, learning, use of resources and so on. There were inspectors allocated to each subject area, and they would present a verbal report to the head on the Friday afternoon, prior to the written report later. Although not the lead inspector for this visit overall, one member of their team was a well-known and much respected person in the educational world, the only one I had ever heard of by name. On this occasion, he was inspecting two things, 'Religious Education' and 'Leadership and Management'.

On that Friday afternoon, I received in turn the verbal reports from the various subject inspectors and as the very last one came, I sat with this venerable person.

'Well, Mr Middlewood, when we come to considering the provision of religious education here, I think it might be appropriate to begin with a two minute silence!'

I swear there was a twinkle in his eye as he said this, and I thought a small grin from me was in order. In essence, I could not have argued with his comment anyway. We then had a discussion which was both fair and friendly, and overall the report which eventually was published was both accurate and encouraging. But I shall never forget that inspector's comment, which gives me the assurance that if there can be a sense of humour expressed in such a witty way by someone at the top of the whole system, then there is hope for all of us who work in it!

PART C
IT'S ALL ACADEMIC ANYWAY

Chapter Six

AMONG THE GREAT AND THE GOOD

After nine years as a school leader, I applied for and was awarded a year's secondment by the Education Authority to carry out research into – the value of teacher secondments! I quite enjoyed the apparent oddity of telling someone that I was on secondment from my school to do research, and when they asked me what I was researching, I could truthfully reply:

'Being on secondment!'

I was able to make my own timetable to carry out the necessary research and I thoroughly enjoyed this year, travelling to different areas of the country, interviewing various personnel who were either currently on secondment or had returned from one. I was based in an outpost centre of the University of Leicester, which was conveniently about

CHAPTER SIX

three hundred metres from my actual home in Northampton! That centre, which is in a nineteenth century building, has since closed and all such outposts moved to the main University campus more than 20 miles away, but at that time, nothing could have been better for me.

One or two people who claim to be friends of mine have unkindly suggested that this closure of the place where I worked might suggest a pattern in my career. Mind you, I have to confess the same thought has entered my own head on occasions. I refer to the fact that out of the number of actual buildings in which I have spent my educational career, at least half have been demolished or taken out of use! The eighteenth century building in the Medway town where I had my second teaching job is no more and only a plaque on a wall there, next to the city's Roman wall, now commemorates a famous alumnus – David Garrick – showing where the school once was. Likewise, the school where I was a headteacher for a decade was also demolished in the 1990s and a well-known local author is commemorated instead by a road entitled 'H E Bates Way'. I might claim it is all coincidence, or that I felt those famous folk needed greater recognition, which is now given, rather than that any memory of me is to be obliterated. Something tells me that I am not that important! If a possible career in helping getting rid of old or unsightly buildings did ever beckon, it is now much too late for that. When I think that even my university where I studied as an undergraduate quickly abandoned its old buildings for new as I arrived, and my first teaching site in higher education now has other uses, it is impossible for me to deny a pattern!

Be that as it may, at the end of my twelve months in that particular building, originally a nineteenth century orphanage, I produced my report for the Local Education Authority with some recommendations for action – just in the month before the national government announced that virtually all teacher secondments were to be abolished!

I decided not to take this decision personally, any more than I took the demolition of those post-Middlewood buildings so, and consoled myself that I had at least gained a second degree qualification from the whole thing, as well as having learned a great deal about research processes, which would, as it turned out, be the basis of my next educational career stage.

At that time, it took me a while to realise that if I were to acquire a second headship or principalship somewhere, the powers there would be expecting me to in effect repeat any success in their school of what I had already achieved in my previous school. After all, one tends to be appointed on one's record. Being ten years older and not necessarily looking for more of the same in my life, I realised that I was not especially wanting to return to any school, and found myself at a career crossroads. Just about then, I was called in for a chat with the senior university tutor who had been looking after me during that year and who ran that Centre. He indicated that it was likely that I could be offered a short-term contract with the university if I so wished, based on the work I had done that year. I expressed pleasure at the prospect, but also some surprise at this since I had not thought my work anything special. Mark looked at me quizzically.

'David,' he said, 'this is Higher Education and this is a university. Some might say you have done something quite remarkable in your time here. It's not your research or the report, although these were good. No, much more importantly, you have actually done what you were asked to do! Moreover, you did it on time. By normal standards in HE, you could well be, and in my opinion are, in the tiny percentage of people who manage to do this. I have waited all year for you to come in and ask for an extension of time to do something, or explain at length why you have not done as much as you would have liked, because there have been various circumstances that have prevented you, etc, etc. You

CHAPTER SIX

haven't and, as I say, that's remarkable in this world!'

No doubt, based on his own long experience in Higher Education, he exaggerated or was being somewhat cynical, but it was clearly based on what he felt to be the norm, and thus it was that I entered upon my new career in Universities on the basis of something that I believe the vast majority of teachers, perhaps people in general, do – simply carry out what they say they will do, and do it when they say they will! I was ready for a new direction in my life and career, and the fact that I only had the security of about two years ahead paid for was something I relished. As it turned out, this new direction became a career which was to last for about a quarter of a century!

So, it was with some excitement that I told my wife that I would be attending a University Education Department staff meeting soon, which on this occasion was to be held at this Centre. Knowing the august company I would be keeping on this lofty occasion, which included professors whose names she knew through her readings on primary education, she was almost as nervous as myself on the day of the eagerly anticipated meeting. The meeting was in the afternoon, and I arrived home at about 5.00pm, to be eagerly greeted by her with a flurry of questions:

'How did it go? Was there lots of debate? Was it mainly curricular or more about student welfare? Did you join in much?'

My reply went something like the following:

'Well, there was certainly some pretty lively debate and argument – I thought some of the people were ready to fall out over things. I think I can say there were three big questions:

1. 'Firstly, when is the university going to make sure there are enough car parking spaces so we do not have to drive round for ages looking for one?
2. 'Secondly, why is that some staff have keys to the resources cupboards, while others do not?
3. 'Thirdly, when are you going to deal with the unfair practice of some senior staff jumping the queue for the work to be photocopied by the technician?'

That was more or less the gist of my report on the first opportunity I had to scale the dizzy intellectual heights of this Olympian gathering of university cultural icons. As to my reply to the question about my own contribution to the debates, I had to confess my answer was – nil!

I do not wish there to be any misunderstanding about this last point. I am as ready as anyone to join in a debate about car parking practices and procedures. In fact, I rather pride myself on having strong, logically formed and coherent opinions on a number of aspects of this important area of human existence, with these views of course being firmly based on evidence. For example, I can hold forth about large vehicles parking in spaces much too small for them, and their drivers complaining that it is the spaces that are the wrong size. As someone who drives a small car, I can assure you I am quite impartial on that matter. My views on those cars with 'Princess on Board' in the rear window not being allowed to park at all, anywhere, because they should really be required to obtain from the Monarch herself some kind of royal permit, are all perfectly logical, I can assure you. I can cogently argue the case for the drivers of cars with such notices being used to argue that the Tower of London might usefully be returned to some of its former uses. I like to display even-handedness in such matters!

CHAPTER SIX

The reason I could not contribute any words of wisdom at the meeting was of course because I had absolutely no knowledge of the parking facilities at the main campus, and had equally no idea where any cupboards, locked or unlocked, were situated. I would have been less confident, I admit, about the queue jumping for the copier, since I had an uneasy feeling that when I had been the head of a school, the relevant technician had put my requests at the front of any queue, whether I requested it or not.

The experience of that first meeting and its similarity to other meetings previously attended clearly affected my judgment of such occasions, and while I went on to attend –and contribute to – numerous group or team meetings over the next eighteen years I spent in Higher Education, I confess to never having attended another full staff meeting in any of the three universities where I have worked –although I was assiduous at sending my apologies and checking that these were recorded in the minutes.

Meetings themselves are something that are always under discussion in education, and those of us who have spent a long time in education would hardly dare to calculate the amount of time that we have spent in them. According to some books on the shelves in bookshops, running an effective meeting is easy! Yet boring and downright bad meetings persist, so that is clearly untrue. I confess to having written about meetings myself and perhaps have only written one really useful thing on the topic. This is of course – do not have a meeting unless you really need to have one! However, they can provide entertainment when you are not too heavily involved. I learned to admire one particular professor at a university where I worked who clearly regarded any meeting as an opportunity for a siesta. They were a chance for him to take time off from his presumably very heavy work schedule. I and a couple of others would watch him as he slowly began to lapse in concentration; his head would droop and finally he would be asleep. I do not mean a doze, but a deep slumber, which even occasionally involved a small snore. We used to amuse ourselves by estimating how long it would take him to nod off, and that helped us pass the time anyway. He was a person of very considerable national, even international, academic repute, and, if the meeting's chairperson should be foolish enough to try to score over him by asking him a question by name on the agenda item being discussed, he would at once open his eyes. More than that, completely unruffled, he would hold forth for two or three minutes on some subject or other, most likely his latest research. This would have absolutely nothing at all to do with the topic under discussion, but no chair ever seemed to challenge him on this irrelevance. The ultimate irony was that when he did occasionally chair a meeting himself, I am told that he was very hard on anyone who did not appear to be attentive! Such is the power of research in Higher Education.

Settling In

I obtained a role in a new Educational Management Development Unit that was being established in the Centre and discovered that my newly appointed professorial boss, Tony, had run in the same London Marathon that I had in the 1980s, which gave us a bond, and he remains a good friend to this day. A hugely busy period of my life then began. This often involved teaching MA students, who were teachers, of course, two or three evenings a week at local Centres, set in Teacher Centres or in schools themselves, and also leading some after-school sessions as well. I was later put in charge of a new initiative, which involved teaching Masters Degree modules to schoolteachers at all levels in their own schools or groups of schools. It was my job to go and negotiate the programmes and then establish them, arrange the details, and I often taught on a good number of them myself. It was work I loved

CHAPTER SIX

and the number of programmes expanded greatly – and quickly! Very soon I found myself travelling not only to neighbouring authorities but further and further afield. As the programme successfully developed and spread geographically, I began to journey by train to some of the more distant outposts. Thus, I have vivid memories of arriving at Plymouth Station, for example, and walking past the blue plaque which informed me that 'Screaming Lord Sutch' had lived there, to stay at a guest house for a night. That station became a regular arrival and departure point for me, as I visited and taught at various schools in the area. We developed a course in the North of England, in Blackburn; this journey involved a change of trains at Preston, so that station became, like Plymouth, etched on my memory, and I particularly liked hearing the announcement about the next train calling at 'Middlewood' (a halt in the Peak District), whilst I awaited the southbound train back home. I vowed to go there but never did, just one of a very small number of regrets of that period. I have, however, a photograph of the halt's sign from a son who did later visit it.

I recall more than one of my former school leader colleagues asking me whether I did not regret or miss the influence that my position as principal had given me at school. One or two even used the word 'power'. The answer was that I certainly did not miss it! I thoroughly enjoyed what I did daily, was almost beguiled by the appreciative feedback I got from these adult learners, and was quite ready to take my place in the queue for any photocopying! I had no ambitions to gain authority over others in Higher Education, although I eventually did take on a responsibility of being Deputy Director of a Leadership Unit. The lighter side of such roles always appealed to me, such as the opportunity to say farewell to a colleague and pull a leg or two. On one such occasion, a very valued friend and colleague was leaving us and I had to say a few words.

After outlining Keith's contribution to the Unit, I said that 'not everyone knows that Keith was once offered the post of Director of Education for the whole of Sky'. Murmurs of admiration and surprise rose in the room as people realised the importance of such a role in a global media giant, and Keith himself sat with a puzzled look.

'But,' I added, 'when he found out there was only one boat a week across to the little island, he turned it down!' Gales of laughter followed and I was pleased with the success of the joke. However, I afterwards reflected how that particular joke could only work in certain geographical contexts. If you didn't know Skye was a small island, known mostly through its boating song, the joke meant nothing. Some of the cockney rhyming slang I had learned in the Kent hop gardens and could sometimes be used to good effect in lectures, would also be incomprehensible in many places, even in some parts of the United Kingdom!

I particularly enjoyed working with support and associate colleagues, who played such a vital role in the Unit's success as they do in every kind of educational establishment. My sense of humour seemed to gel with several of them, as it had in my Deputy Principal days. The key as always is to have a sense of who will be keen to laugh and to judge when as well as with whom. In times when sensitivities can be easily offended, this 'nose' for the right person and time is crucial. For example, when Pip, our senior administrator, brought a newly appointed person along to meet me, as she would be working for me (I always preferred working 'with' me), we happened to meet in the corridor.

I saw a tiny woman – well under five feet – with Pip, who said:

'This is Clem Little, the new secretary.'

CHAPTER SIX

I mean – 'Mrs LITTLE'! Who could resist a comment?

I concluded three things that would make a joke here acceptable:

1. she had a huge smile on her face
2. she must have endless comments in her life so far on this situation and was still grinning
3. as she was married, she obviously had the sense of humour which chose a man called Little whose name she would take!

So I leapt in – at the deep end, perhaps?

'Nice to meet you, Clem. I am sure we'll get on very well – but you know, you don't have to get on your knees every time we meet! Oh, sorry, you aren't on your knees, I see!'

Clem burst out laughing and said,

'I can see we are going to get along very well!'

And we did for the two years she was with us. Tragically, she died of cancer some years later, but her widower remains a friend of myself and my wife and he tells often of how Clem told him regularly that those two years with me formed one of the most enjoyable periods of her working life.

I sometimes made a point of reminding myself of my good fortune in the work I was doing at that stage of my life and career. It might have been just getting older, but I have always argued that when things, especially the little ones, are going well, we need to relish them. The majority of life, after all, is made up of myriad small occasions, and not of grand events. It is certainly a philosophy Jacqui and I have always shared, and so I would sometimes stop on a drive to a school on a pleasant spring or summer's day before an evening session, get out the car and look at a scene that had caught my eye, reflecting on how good things were for me at that time, and perhaps even saying to myself, 'AND you are getting paid for this!'

On that subject, my contracts were always fixed-term, and latterly part-time, an arrangement which suited me well, and one that saw me through the whole of my career in Higher Education. I could feel that some of the time I had was really mine and I could decide how I used it. I remember walking through an area on my way from an underground station to a school in Walthamstow in London, and discovering a tiny museum of local history. I noted its limited opening times and arrived in good time for the next session to enable me to spend a delightful thirty minutes there, learning so much about the people and customs of the region. Some of this I was then able to use in the sessions at the school there, including knowledge of some old local customs which seemed comical today, such as putting a schoolteacher in the stocks when it was found that he had committed a blasphemy! Some of the local teachers had never heard of this, which is so often the way. It is the incidentals in life that so often give us a relish for what that life can offer, just as in school, it was not the huge success in examinations of one's students that gave the greatest pleasure, but the incidental mumbled thanks of a school ne'er do well, or a genuine apology from a penitent rogue.

Not every context I was sent to was aesthetically pleasing, of course, and one in particular had its disturbing elements. Having been contacted by the acting headteacher of a specialschool in the Oxford area, I drove to the school to investigate the possibility of setting up a programme there. Arriving in the playground area, the first thing that I noticed was a police car outside the entrance. I had often seen police cars on

CHAPTER SIX

school premises before – but not one with the windscreen smashed in! I nervously left my car nearby and, not liking to ask about the police vehicle, my discussions with the acting Head got under way. We agreed to set up a course and I told Mark that I had a colleague who was an expert in special education and that he would be working with me on the programme. I then found my own car intact and drove home safely afterwards.

I sold the idea to this colleague, John, without mentioning the police car, of course, and we visited the school together for the first session. Shortly after that, John emigrated to New Zealand and has never returned to England except for a short visit. Personally, I confess I always felt that to be rather an extreme way of indicating that he did not want to participate in the course there! However, John wrote amusingly and good-naturedly in his farewell piece in the Unit's Newsletter about how he had been 'lured' by me to Oxford. With 'dreams of spires and punts on rivers', he wrote, he had gone with me and found the reality rather different, as indeed it was. I have never been sure as to the degree to which the story about the police car windscreen and his wish to go to New Zealand were connected!

However, the extracurricular skills developed at this school for emotionally and behaviourally challenged pupils, to use the correct terminology of the time, proved invaluable on one occasion. I got over my initial nervousness as the course got underway, and found the staff wonderfully committed to study, as the dedicated professionals they were. But it must have been nerves which made me one day fairly early on in the programme do something I had never done before or have done since –I locked myself out of my car! I had just arrived at the school and could only look miserably through the car window at the keys inside. Feeling a complete fool, I sheepishly reported this to the first teacher I met and said I would have to summon the AA. She looked at me in pitying amazement at my naivety, then looked through the door of the nearest classroom.

'Er, you, Sean. Come here please and help this nice gentleman.'

Sean, a fifteen year old with eyes firmly fixed floorwards, shuffled forward, and raised those eyes just enough to show me what a nuisance I was, and glowered at me.

'This man comes here to help us with our work so we can all help you. He's locked out of his car, so can you please sort him out?'

Sean looked at me, as one would look at some lowly creature hardly worth giving a second glance, shrugged his shoulders and said,

'Okay – but I'll need my stuff.'
'Go to the office then and get it, please.'

Sean went to the office and returned with a piece of something metallic in his hand and asked where the car was. He followed me to the car, reached to the driver's door handle with the metallic object and almost at once, I heard the click and the door was opened. I regained my keys and then locked the car as we left it. I later realised what a futile gesture that last action had been! We returned and while I thanked Sean profusely, his look suggested that it was more a case of his taking pity on me than of performing an act of helpfulness! Trying to make conversation with him, I suggested, only half seriously, that he might like to teach me how he had opened my car so easily. This got his attention, as I think he weighed up the possibility of my proving to be any kind of useful addition to his circle of friends. I don't think, however, that he was much impressed by my potential. His answer eventually was along the lines of:

CHAPTER SIX

'I could show you, but I dunno. I'll see.'

It was, I think, quite a polite rejection – or do I count that as another failed application, I wonder?

My admiration for his teachers increased even more. As I recall, he did not take the metallic object back to the school office that day, but I did not hear of a spate of car offences at all, so I kept quiet. The incident also confirmed some of my theories about learning – there are some 'life skills' that they do not teach you on the official curriculum!

Another embarrassing incident on my travels to centres in England happened when I was on an overnight Friday and Saturday trip to a school in Blackburn, where I was leading an MA course. Sometimes, I stayed overnight at Preston, where I changed trains, but occasionally stayed a night in Blackburn itself, as on this trip. A very efficient secretary had booked a guest house near the station, and after the Friday evening session, one of the teachers dropped me off from her car at the given address. I rang the bell and went in. The service was slow and the welcoming landlord, if that is what he was, seemed slightly suspicious, as if I were being weighed up. However, I was tired and it was late, so I retired to my room, having checked breakfast time in the morning. At about eleven at night, a knock on my door was followed by a woman's voice, asking me if I was 'Okay in there?' and whether there was anything else I needed. I called out that I was fine, and fell asleep. Through the night, the place seemed rather noisy, with a lot of movement, conversation and occasional laughter, so I did not sleep deeply.

I woke in the morning, washed and shaved and got my bag and papers all ready for my next session at the school, so that I could leave straight after breakfast for the school, as my first tutorial was at 9.30 there. No one could be found anywhere in the hotel! I searched in the dining room and the kitchen, but found nobody! I was cursing the place's inefficiency and virtually resigned to missing any breakfast and getting ready to get my bag and leave, when the person who had let me in the previous evening slouched into the kitchen.

'You're around early!' was his greeting.

Crossly, I explained I needed breakfast in a hurry because I had to leave very soon.

'None of the girls are up yet,' he remarked. I didn't see this as any kind of an answer to my request for a breakfast, unless there were several girls who were chefs who were all oversleeping. In fact, his comment was something of a non-sequitur until a light bulb flashed in my head. 'Girls!' The noises in the night, the activities through the night! What kind of establishment was this, I wondered? In fact, I did not wonder; I was stone cold certain that it was the kind of place that has had many names over the years, but above all it was one which, if my name was associated with it, would bring me the kind of notoriety that no university could desire. It is not true that there is no such thing as bad publicity! I now remembered that and realised why no one had asked me to sign a register last evening. Well, thank goodness, there would be no record of my stay! I hastily said that I was no longer hungry, and would be leaving at once as I was late. I gave some cash to the man for my room, and brushed aside any offer he might have been going to make of a receipt. The door slammed behind me and I hurried the mile to the school, trying to calm myself on the way. Now that I was safe, I started to see the funny side. It would make a good story back at the University Centre. Or would it? On reflection, I decided to say nothing there, and when I was back at base on the Monday and asked by the secretary how the trip had gone, I simply remarked that it was fine, but:

CHAPTER SIX

'That place you booked wasn't very good at all. Don't use that one again, please'.

She replied that she was sorry but it had 'looked very nice' on the website, to which I replied that the room had been okay but the service had not been what I expected. That at least was true, and confirmed that my decision not to tell the whole story was a correct one. My wife remains the only one I told that tale to – until now of course!

One-to-One

One of the key features of teaching on these programmes was the need to provide individual tutorials for each student about the written assignment they were required to submit. I discovered that I was surprisingly good at these, or so I have been told by staff and students alike. Since these one-to-one sessions were bringing two adults together, they sometimes almost became counselling sessions, since the men or women concerned often needed to tell you about the circumstances both at school and aften at home under which they did the work. Occasionally, some would have heartbreaking tales to share and I always tried to give as much help as possible and give as much sympathy and empathy as I could. Bereavements, divorces, house moving, births, all were part of life's pattern and I have given tutorials under all kinds of circumstances, including eleven month old twins crawling on the floor around my feet while Mum and I worked out her next piece of work! As someone who so greatly admired anyone who could teach during the day and then pursue study afterwards, those people had no greater supporter than myself. Only very occasionally did such things cause me problems, but I do recall the situation involving Paul and Wendy vividly!

Paul and Wendy were a married couple, each following the Masters course with myself as tutor, but at separate centres, as each was headteacher of a primary school in two different Midlands towns, only about ten miles apart. After two years, I had got to know each of them well and would usually inquire about the other when tutoring one of them. We had reached the dissertation and therefore the final stage of the Masters programme with both, which involved tutorials only. At one such tutorial, I asked Paul as usual how his wife was, and he, rather uncomfortably, answered that they were 'splitting up'. I said how sorry I was to hear that, and went to my next tutorial with Wendy the following week with appropriate words in mind.

'Sorry to hear about you and Paul. Sad, but of course these things do happen.'

Her reply did not suggest any kind of resignation to what fate may have cruelly allotted her, however.

'Yes! Well, he went off with that cow, Jenny Watson, you know!'

I had not known that, but I DID know Jenny Watson because she was a member of my other tutor group, the one Paul was in! Was I being accused of being responsible for the whole thing? And what was to be said to Jenny Watson the next time she and I had a tutorial?

'Anyway, I'll show him I don't need him,' Wendy went on. 'I'll find myself a new man and someone higher up than him, you see!'

Was she looking at me? Surely not! I averted my eyes and hastily brought the topic round to my wife having been a primary headteacher herself and how I knew what a hard job it was and so on.

CHAPTER SIX

The next few months had their uncomfortable moments, and I realised that there was a fierce competition going on between Paul and Wendy over completing their dissertations first and, of course, more importantly, gaining a higher award than the other at the end. Each enquired about the other's progress, although not in any spirit of putting the past behind them, whilst Jenny Watson said never a word on the whole matter and made steady progress herself. Wendy made a point of never mentioning Paul or Jenny by name. She would say:

'And how is HE getting on? Badly, I hope!'
'And I suppose SHE is doing alright? Huh!'

and other such helpful remarks. I occasionally felt what it would be like to be a solicitor representing both sides in an acrimonious dispute, and I no longer looked forward to those particular tutorials. I mused over the consequences of the various possible permutations of the degree results of the three of them, whilst always stressing to them individually that their results did not depend solely on my assessment! When the results were eventually published, I noticed that Jenny had obtained the highest grade of all three of them, whilst Paul and Wendy had obtained exactly the same mark. I felt something of relief at their dead heat, as I had a feeling I would have been unjustly accused by the 'loser', had there been one. I wondered what implications, if any, this might have had for the futures of all three of them. Their thank you letters to me were very pleasant but told me no more! I have, however, no feeling that this was a story with a happy ending!

HMI – Again!

One other thing that occurred during my visits to school-based MA sessions was that I found I had been chosen again for a visit by HMI.

As I was not now in a leadership role, this disturbed me much less than many of my departmental colleagues. In the inspection of the University's Education Department, the teaching or delivery ('delivery' was the word of the moment) of MA programmes was a focus, and the Inspectorate apparently had a special interest in those being taught on school premises. Thus, I was 'warned' that an HMI would visit my session in a particular week, which happened to be at a secondary school in a Warwickshire town. The students were alerted, and I assured them that the visitor's focus was not on them. Being used to inspections themselves, they were fully supportive of me, and I prepared my two and a half hour session on one of my favourite topics about which I had both researched and published, 'Recruitment and Selection', as part of the module on Leading and Managing Human Resources.

Determined not to change my normal style, I began my evening, the Inspector ensconced at the back of the room, with a slide full of cartoons! This needs explaining! During my time as Head of a school, I had received an application for the post of Head of Music which contained a CV, presented in the form of a comic strip. I had invited the sender for interview and wondered whether he might arrive in a funny hat or clown's garb. However, he arrived dressed in the formal clothing appropriate for an interview, and at the end of the process, we had appointed him. I later learned how many times that CV had been rejected elsewhere. With his permission, and anonymously of course, I was often able to use this CV to spark a conversation about whether the teachers would or would not have called him for interview, the purpose of any discussion being to bring out the prejudices that all of us carry about the appearances of other persons. As had happened when I had used this previously, the group split about fifty-fifty on this and this division led to an excellent debate about those prejudices that we all hold and how these can show themselves in the managing of selection processes, unless you are prepared to recognise your having such prejudices.

CHAPTER SIX

I was able to add in various anecdotes about the Chair of Governors I once had who believed that any man with a beard was not to be trusted, and a beard AND glasses almost certainly signified that he was a communist spy! Some students were doubtful of this tale until I quoted from a memo (anonymous again, of course) that I had retained which showed that I was only very slightly exaggerating. When I added yet another example, I noticed the Inspector scribbling furiously. I wondered if I was being dismissed as a hopelessly lightweight lecturer and that my career in Higher Education was nearing its end. If so, I decided I would go out in a blaze of glory! Thus, after rounding off the session, I asked them about how they had parked when arriving that evening and, cheekily, included the Inspector in the survey! The story was about governors who observed interviewees arriving and noting whether they reversed their cars in the spaces or drove in front first. Having got the results, I was able to tell the reversing group that they would not have got that job, because those governors thought that anyone reversing in was only thinking how quickly they could get away after school on a normal day! The Inspector, by the way, was one of those who, like me, would not have got the job!

She asked to speak to me after the session had ended and we walked out together to the car park. Our conversation there lasted over 30 minutes and she closely questioned me about the various stories I had told.

'Fascinating!' she said. 'I have got to do a report on Governors' roles in school appointments and that was really useful. Thank you so much! I shall use some of your tales, but of course they will be unattributed.'

Thus, instead of a two-minute silence this time, I had a half-hour thank you! Sometimes indeed, the fates are with you! In my whole career, I have received two visits from Her Majesty's Inspectorate, and on both occasions, I got someone with a sense of humour! Or perhaps I misjudge them and merely follow the stereotype of the serious suited civil servant? Perhaps in reality, their meetings and training sessions are packed with innuendo and cracking jokes? We will never know until one of them writes a book like this one, and that is not likely, given legal security requirements imposed on them. But just for a moment, we can enjoy the fantasy of a group of HMIs maybe throwing custard pies and dropping their trousers!

Writing

I have not mentioned that it was through working in Higher Education that my published writings began. Thanks to Tony, I was a co-editor with him (in reality more of an assistant editor on that first occasion!) in the first of a series of books published by our unit, about managing people in education. The series was very successful in publishing terms and the chapters I had contributed to the book very well received. It was the first of more than twenty books published over the next twenty-plus years, many with Tony, and later with Ian Abbott. I hardly like to recall that some of the early books made references to 'Human Resources', an ugly phrase in my view, and the change to 'Managing People' was a big improvement to this particular teacher of English! Human Resources departments of course exist in many large organisations including universities and, sadly, do not enjoy universal affection. Now I think of it, the HRM department of the third and final university in which I worked never did issue me with a P45 Certificate, despite three requests, so I suppose it is possible that I am technically employed there still!

I was asked to become the editor of a new practitioner journal for school leaders in secondary education, where the emphasis was to be on actual practice rather than academic theory. I felt I needed someone to help me who was actually doing the job at that time, and I persuaded

CHAPTER SIX

Richard, a friend and former colleague of mine from my English Department days, to become co-editor. He had, since those days, gone on to secure a headship in the same region as I lived. That journal was quickly followed by a primary version and this time another close friend, Paul, a primary headteacher, joined me, and the three of us enjoyed several train journeys together to and from London which were both productive and highly amusing at times, including some reminiscences.

One of these reminiscences brought back to both Richard and I the memory of our first meeting. When I had been Head of English, we advertised for a teacher to be second in the Department and Richard had applied and been invited for interview at the school. He had arrived and we had spent the morning informally, and, it has to be said, getting on famously. We were both feeling that we would be able to work together pretty well. The formal interview was to be in the afternoon, but during the lunchtime, I met Richard in the gents' lavatory by chance and he was looking worried. He explained that the zip on his trousers had just broken and he was acutely embarrassed about the forthcoming interview. We went to the school office, explained the situation to a secretary, who kindly supplied him with a safety pin to hold things together, so to speak. We agreed that the pin ought to suffice for the present.

The interview duly took place and it was clear that Richard was the best candidate. While he waited outside, the Headteacher and I conferred. I stated that in my view that he was the best person and he was my choice to be appointed. The head seemed to be just slightly hesitant.

'Look,' he said, 'you are the head of the subject and I do overall agree with you anyway that he is the best, but I do have one query.'

'What's that?' I asked.

'Do you not think he can be a very tense, wound-up sort of person? Did you not notice how, throughout the whole interview, he was leaning forward, with his legs crossed, as if he couldn't bear to sit upright?'

I managed to persuade the head that it was possibly just interview nerves! Richard was appointed, and went on in a pretty relaxed way to loftier things in education! I know he has subsequently always been appreciative of school secretaries wherever he worked, as I have, and as all leaders should be. Whether he keeps that safety pin as a memento, I must remember to ask him one day!

Further Travels

One special opportunity that came to me through working in Higher Education was that of travelling abroad to teach and/or research, and some of the countries I 'discovered' were South Africa, New Zealand, Greece, and Seychelles among others. My connection with Greece had actually begun when my beloved stepdaughter, Samantha, settled in Crete by marrying Apostolos and later providing myself and Jacqui with a granddaughter and a grandson. Veatriki and George, of course, were bilingual from the start and it was this that spurred me to enter a formal adult learning situation as a student by enrolling for a class in 'Beginners Greek'. It was fun being back in the classroom again, especially as my new classmates comprised a wide range of people, from those simply wanting to know how to ask for a beer while on holiday, those likely to work there, and family members with relations abroad. This diversity was enjoyable, although the dropout rate was alarming, with the class size dropping from seventeen to about six in a month! I was fortunate in having a good knowledge of grammar, but one or two

CHAPTER SIX

perfectly intelligent people were handicapped by having been at school during the time when teaching grammar was unfashionable and I felt sorry for them, as it was no fault of theirs. I myself made reasonable progress, kept up to the mark by being regularly tested on the phone by two very young Cretans who wanted to know if 'Grandad was good in class'! My wife of course reported that I was by far the naughtiest pupil, a charge I strenuously denied.

Given this link with Greece, a smattering of vocabulary, and a lack of fear about making a fool of myself if I got something wrong in the language, it came about that I presented a paper at a Conference in Athens, later followed by an invitation to teach at a university there for a week in January, which I did for about six years altogether. It was there I gained my awareness of a different concept of time that exists (I found it in Africa too), quite unlike that with which I had grown up. I have grown to love the Greeks as a friendly, and cheerful people, and my teaching sessions there were hugely enjoyable for me, and, I am certain, for my students. They certainly seemed to enjoy them. They were not used to such humour from visiting lecturers and I used my smattering of their language to good effect. I carefully prepared a nice little five-minute speech in Greek which I gave at the beginning, saying that I had family in Crete and would teach in English and so on. This was always accepted with smiling admiration and even applause at times. We all admire someone who makes an effort to learn our own language. Of course, each group I had did not realise that I gave exactly the same speech to them as I had to the previous one! They were more used to being lectured at in the actual sessions, but adjusted well to being asked to discuss topics in groups. They loved being teased about the Greek approach to time, so by the second year, when I had adjusted to being collected from my hotel at the very time I was officially due to begin my lecture, I always began thus, after my short introduction in Greek:

'Now, do you want to operate on English time or Greek time please? In English time, we will start at the stated hour, take a short break in the middle, and finish at the correct time. In Greek time, we shall start about twenty minutes after the official time, take a long break in the middle and finish about fifteen minutes early!' They would all howl out delightedly:

'Greek time!' I would give the required shoulder shrug and off we'd go. It enabled us all to mock both the North European apparent inflexibility and the more laid back attitude of the South European. It seemed to work well, as I was regularly asked to return the next year.

The more relaxed attitude there also showed itself in the way I was paid in the early years, before the Euro Crisis came about for the Greek economy. By this time my employment by my own university was on a seventy-five per cent contract, leaving me free to earn elsewhere in the rest of my time, such as on the trips to Athens. On my first visit, Anna, my Greek friend at the University, said we needed to get my payment sorted and took me to the administrator's office. I signed a form, although I could not read it (my Greek was not yet that proficient) and was then given an envelope – filled with euro notes! It was all perfectly official and above board but not something I have encountered at an institutional level in education, anywhere else in the world. It was the source of much ribaldry when I returned home to England, especially from my very good friend and colleague, Ian. My saving grace was that the envelope I had been given was white, and not the brown one synonymous with under the counter dealings! The system changed two years later, after the Greek euro 'bail out' and things went to the opposite extreme, with receipts having to be issued for everything, even a packet of sweets or a newspaper. When Ian Abbott joined me on some later visits, he was always slightly peeved that he was not paid via the 'white envelope system', as he always called it.

CHAPTER SIX

I had got to know Ian, who was to become one of my closest friends, when our university took over a contract to provide MA programmes for school leaders in Seychelles, the smallest African nation and of course an island state. It meant twice a year (usually January and May) going to that country's capital, Victoria, and teaching a group several modules in a very concentrated programme of lectures and tutorials. I had done a couple of these and Ian joined me on the third. We hit it off immediately and got to know each other's quirks and odd sense of humour during those times. It led to writing books together, collaborative research, and an enduring friendship. It was with Ian, in fact, to whom the students referred when they inquired if I was going on the stage in a double act after retirement from teaching in Higher Education.

The people of the Seychelles are, like the Greeks, a delightful, friendly and appreciative race, and greatly enjoyed having humour as a key ingredient of their learning. The students were committed and conscientious, and took their studies seriously but they also loved to laugh. What more can any teacher want! They were mostly devout and also loved a cheeky comment, even risqué, but never crude! A particular shared cornerstone of the humour was their famous Coco de Mer! Now, the coco de mer is a kind of nut, which only grows in the Seychelles. Trying to describe it is not easy, however. As you know, virtually all plants have a male and female version, as has the coco de mer. The best way to put it is that the coco de mer has the most obviously visual and physically expressed differences between the male and the female versions, very explicit indeed. From this description, you should have worked out the shapes of the aforesaid plant. The male is comparatively rare. As I sit writing this in my 'den', I can see one of my most treasured possessions – a large coco de mer – very obviously female! – which I was presented with by a Seychelles graduate cohort. The message with it reads:

'To Professor David Middlewood
With thanks for his wonderful teaching – and humour!'

It is not only valued by me but is a source of discussion with visitors and of endless amusement for small grandchildren! They always referred to it as 'Grandad's bottom', before they grew old enough to realise the finer details of the coco de mer.

The final two words of the students' message explain everything that I am saying here. When I gave a speech at a farewell graduation dinner in Victoria for Ian and myself, I announced – with a straight face of course – that the MA letters that they could now put after their names actually stood for 'Middlewood and Abbott'! and they seemed to find this riotously amusing.

Naturally, going to the Seychelles twice a year was viewed by university colleagues as a kind of sinecure, despite our protestations about the amount of work involved – I have never had so many offers of assistance during my whole career! The intimacy of such a small nation is disarming. Where else can you say to someone in any part of the country, that you'll meet them at 'THE pub' or arrange to stand by 'THE traffic lights'?

There being only one set of traffic lights in the whole town, and indeed in the country, you might imagine that there would be special respect for road crossings in the Seychelles. I once foolishly made the mistake of assuming these striped markings on the road indicated it was a safe place to cross. Halfway across, I realised that the fast-approaching car was NOT slowing down and had to hurtle myself out of its path, to the accompaniment of choice words from the driver asking me if I was actually trying to kill myself!

CHAPTER SIX

Such offers of help from colleagues to assist me were less forthcoming with visits to certain other countries of course. I had first visited South Africa in the late 1990s, for research purposes, and have returned on several occasions, managing on one occasion to combine a conference speech with the wedding of Tony to Chabala near Johannesburg. That country was and is fascinating, and particularly so in that period after the new Republic came into being in 1994. I learned so much in those early visits, especially seeing the hunger for learning from schoolchildren of all ages, remarkable given the dire circumstances under which so many black pupils existed at school. I remember one of the most moving moments of my whole life being a brief chat with a black woman in her mid-nineties who told me she could be content to die, now that she had managed to cast her first vote in those first national elections, having queued for four hours to do so. As with the children's thirst for schooling in often wretched conditions, it was, of course, so sobering to reflect on how much we privileged folk of Western developed nations not only take for granted but often grow to disdain.

There were, however, plenty of lighter moments also. Our group was centred on the Province of KwaZulu Natal and we stayed in Durban. It was there we first encountered the concept of time that is so close to the Southern European one.

Having a meeting arranged at the University at two in the afternoon, we four English academics arrived at just before then and awaited our South African counterparts. At twenty past two, the relevant professor of the university arrived and started to chat. When we inquired about the other attendees, he replied that they 'would be along'. Then it dawned on him!

'Ah, I forgot. Sorry. This is an afternoon meeting and they will be here this afternoon okay. This is African time – you'll get used to it!'

We tried to get used to it and – I have to say – with mixed success. Not enough to prepare me for the first conference at which I was to present a paper in Athens. When my wife and I arrived at the university for the scheduled 9.00am (we were combining it with a visit to the family), we could find no one, and began to think we had got the wrong site, when a helpful site janitor assured us that it WAS the correct place and things would get going 'soon'! I think I can say on this occasion, we did learn pretty quickly, spending an extra half hour in bed each morning, although always with a nagging doubt about being late!

This issue of time is, of course, not just a cultural one, but in education very much a professional one, as in many walks of life. I confess to being, if anything, a bit obsessive about being on time for arranged engagements, and fortunately my wife is the same – although she would say not as much as me. In my own family, two of my sons have, shall we say, a more relaxed attitude to what the words 'being on time' mean, whereas my son Philip, along with his wife, is just like me and my wife, and we usually joke about being '30 seconds late'! Yet, none of the late-minded in the family would dream of being late for work – for them, home and work clearly exist in two different universes. As a teacher and particularly as a school leader, lateness of staff was complete anathema to me, something I could not understand or tolerate in teachers. I recall one teacher who, if in a conversation with me at break time, would try to prolong the talk, even though a class would be waiting. I tried hints and firm statements but only cured him by action. The lesson bell had gone and he stayed with me, so I started walking with him alongside. After a while, he asked me where I was heading and I told him the particular classroom.

CHAPTER SIX

'That's mine!' he said.
'Oh. That's why I'm going there.'
'But I haven't picked up my books yet!'
'You wouldn't have had time, surely?'
'No, I suppose not.'

We reached the room, and the noise ceased. I apologised to the students for delaying Mr J and said it was my fault. The teacher entered the room, shamefaced but grateful in one sense, and gave what I assume was a very good, and probably more spontaneous lesson than normal. I do not recall him delaying again in conversations with me, after that. In fact, now I think about it, I do not recall him seeking all that many conversations with me at all.

At university level, whilst some lecturers were a little relaxed about punctuality, most were extremely conscientious about arriving on time. As for myself, as I was teaching school teachers, it was important for me to continue what I had done in schools in this practice, and being punctual was no hardship for me. In any case, I would always argue that it is much better to start bang on time and then, if you finish just a little earlier than the set time, your audience will forgive you and may even thank you! If you have been boring, they'll be glad of an early finish; if you have been enthralling, you will leave them crying out for more!

Chapter Seven

A VERY BRIEF LOOK BACK – AND FORWARD

Coming Right Up To Date – But Not Very!

Although I am no longer employed as a professional teacher either at school or university, I am not so sure that it is possible to stop being a teacher. One of the things that is said is that you can always tell a teacher because of the way they will point or wag a finger, even in a social context! My wife and I were both conscious of this when we got together and we tried hard to avoid this habit. I think we succeeded, but whether impartial witnesses would agree, I am not completely sure. Certainly, I believe what is inherent is much less the urge to tell than the desire to help – that, of course, is true of any profession in the social or

CHAPTER SEVEN

caring fields. There are definitely some aspects of the educational world that I shall always miss, and some that I am glad not to be there whilst they develop. One of the latter for me certainly is the much greater emphasis on digital technology.

I am what is commonly known in the modern world as relatively 'low tech'. What is even more of a crime to a small number of my acquaintances is that I actually like being so! I have no interests in gadgetry, use no social media, and my mobile phone has no apps. As I tell anyone who asks, I use my limited phone for telephoning (and the occasional text). My reasons for disliking some particular digital devices are, naturally, in my opinion, well founded. For example, my dislike of sat navs comes from the fact that various visitors to the Victorian terraced house where I live with my wife, such as delivery personnel, or service engineers, have arrived, usually late, and say, always in an annoyingly accusing tone:

'Your house isn't on my sat nav!' The conversation always goes thus:
'I think you mean your sat nav failed to find this house.'
'What's the difference?'

'Well, this house has been here for a century and a half. How long has your sat nav been around? You can't expect Victorian builders to have anticipated everything!'

A pause follows.

'Well, I'm here now anyway.'

I cannot dispute their presence, of course.

And my deliberate avoidance of self-service places in supermarkets is shown in the answer I give to the person (who could be serving anyway!) who asks me if I would like to use one, is always,

'No thanks.'
'Why not?'
'I am thinking about your job.'

I would blame nobody if, on reading this, they attributed it all to that trait of stubbornness which I have previously acknowledged. But if I am honest, I admit that I genuinely have no curiosity about gadgets and contrivances. As I type these words and stop and look at the keyboard, I can see at least thirty buttons to press that I have absolutely no idea what they do. Similarly, on the very rare occasions I have bought a new car, I normally say:

'I'll have the same one as the one I've just had.'

Of course, when I get in the new vehicle, I find that the dashboard has annoyingly been altered since the last model and I have to explore where the familiar things I need are, but there still are in a car I have had for four years a number of knobs and buttons whose function I have no concept of.

BUT – if I come across a new word in a book or crossword, I cannot rest until I have found its origin, its variants and everything else about it (in a dictionary, of course). If I find a reference to a hitherto unknown writer (usually a minor one of the past), I feel compelled to find out everything I can about her or him, what else they wrote, and often have to go out and find some of those lost folk's works. It is very similar with a painter or dancer. Similarly, I am fascinated by trying to work out why people think and act the way they do, and why animal and plant life operate as they do. So many areas of life fascinate me, yet not gadgets. We truly are, and it is such a truism, all different!

Because of my long involvement in education, I have the greatest respect for any kind of learning and believe everyone is capable of talent in some area. I deeply resent the idea that some people are much 'cleverer' than others in that universal sense in which some people use the word. In schooling, this has often meant a particular kind of talent is valued above other kinds, and this is often overrated. Of course, people like myself have done well out of this (I earlier noted how my memory helped me with examination success at school), but that does not mean it is right. I have had conversations with skilled people who say something like,

'But you are clever',

to which I reply that I am clever in one particular area as they are clever in whatever it is they are doing, assembling a motorcycle, dismantling a boiler, repairing a lock or whatever. And when I think of the former pupil I mentioned in the preface to the book, I know that my life would be in a complete mess if people like him did not empty my waste bins! Of course, I realise I may be prejudiced in favour of bin collectors because of my own father's experience, but I know I shall always value their work.

If some of this makes me appear a technological dinosaur, you might console yourself with the knowledge of what happened to the dinosaurs eventually! More seriously, of course, I am never against digital technology per se; it is just that I am not one of those people who think it is the answer to everything. In fact, just like we human beings, it is part of the solution as well as part of the cause of the planet's problems today. During the lockdowns in 2020 and 2021, I began to realise that there were some people who actually preferred contact by Zoom to real face-to-face human contact and that worries me hugely. However, we humans do have one great advantage over all forms of digital technology – WE have a sense of humour! I do not find many of my friends chuckling at or with their machines, only at people's use or misuse of them. People are much more likely to be found cursing the gadgetry when it goes wrong, rather than enjoying a joke with it. In fact, I have found on those occasions that even my more expert friends tend to adopt a similar strategy to mine, for example, switching the device off and refusing to talk with it for a while, believing contact will resume later satisfactorily. Other phrases I employ and have heard used by others include:

'Okay, well, be like that, you stupid thing!'
'I'm going to give you one more chance!'
'Giving you a good kick looks like the best bet!'

Occasionally, even an expert can try softer tactics, such as:

'Oh, come on now. You can do it.'

And even pleading:

'Now, don't let me down now!'

What I never hear is the expert being jokey with the gadget, hence my belief in the superiority of humans!

Although I lag in the modern digital world, I can claim to be completely up to date in the world of global families at least. Not only do I have the Greek connections already mentioned, including a granddaughter who is a professional footballer playing in England, but one of my sons

CHAPTER SEVEN

has lived in Australia for more than twenty years, and I have another granddaughter who lives in South Africa. I remember vividly whilst being on a research visit to New Zealand, my wife (who accompanied me) and I decided to visit my son, James, in Sydney. Thus we could truly say we had been to Australia for a weekend! All these opportunities came thanks to my being in education. When I consider that my own mother never in her lifetime travelled north of London, some of these changes really are remarkable.

While reflecting on digital worlds, it is perhaps hard for my grandchildren's generation to realise the crucial importance of actual human social contact and, just as I failed to interest myself enough in my grandparents' earlier lives, why should they want to know of mine? I took for granted that when I visited my mother's parents that their delicious fresh drinking water came from a well in the garden, after all. It certainly sounds at least nineteenth century practice. Having lived in a cottage as a small boy, where we fetched the coal from the cellar beneath the sitting room (the only room!), I tried to describe this aspect of my childhood to my grandson, Max, when he was about six years old. Having obviously just studied a particular era at school, he asked me:

'Was that in the Tudor times?'!

I suppose it might as well have been, and even my early school and teaching days may now seem so. Whilst today's schools are indeed different, learning – the main point of their existence – remains central, and I am as convinced as ever that learning can only ever be effective if it is enjoyable – and what can make it more enjoyable than a touch of humour? If the awful lockdowns of 2020 and 2021 taught us anything as far as education is concerned, it is that online learning is no substitute for real face-to-face schooling. This is because schools – and colleges and universities – offer so many forms of social contact and interaction which we all crave as humans, and humour remains an essential ingredient in all such activity. I do not claim that effective learning is not possible without humour; some vital learning may be a rather serious slog at times. What I do maintain is that a commitment to learning will only play its part in contributing to a full human life if it contains a good proportion of humorous enjoyment in what is happening around you. Or, looking at it the other way round, when you have a good laugh at something in life, I am willing to bet that you learn something as well!

A Footnote.

This has been, of course, a highly selective account of a life, where I have chosen to focus on the many humorous events I have encountered in my work. Of course, many other things have occurred outside of work in a life which has had its share of romance, passion, pleasure and scandal, as well as occasional sorrow and setbacks, although never any regrets! The first twenty years and the most recent forty years of my life have brought me at a personal level the most happiness and fulfilment, much of it described in poems I have written and published elsewhere. However, through it all, the people I taught and worked with remained the bedrock for whatever else I did. Thus, it seemed right to give it and them their place in the spotlight in this book.

ACKNOWLEDGEMENTS

Obviously, this book draws on memories of experiences shared with many people, friends and fellow professionals. There are good friends outside of education, of course, but for this book my thanks go to so many people that I have taught and worked with. These include, in no particular order, Ian Abbott, Paul Rangecroft, Richard Parker, Tony Bush, Howard Horsley, Michael Pennington, the late Bob Horgan, the late Ken Dodsworth, the late Tony Pulford, and friends since boyhood such as Doug Sedge, Allen Earl and John Waterman. These all happen to be male, so I am glad to save my very special thanks to three special women, including my late mother without whom I would have achieved little, and my sister, Daphne, for her unfailing love and loyalty. My greatest thanks of course are to my wife, Jacqui, who has not only shared her teaching and other school experiences with me, but has shared everything else and made this book possible.

www.ingramcontent.com/pod-product-compliance
Lightning Source LLC
Chambersburg PA
CBHW060154050426
42446CB00013B/2813